AF504400

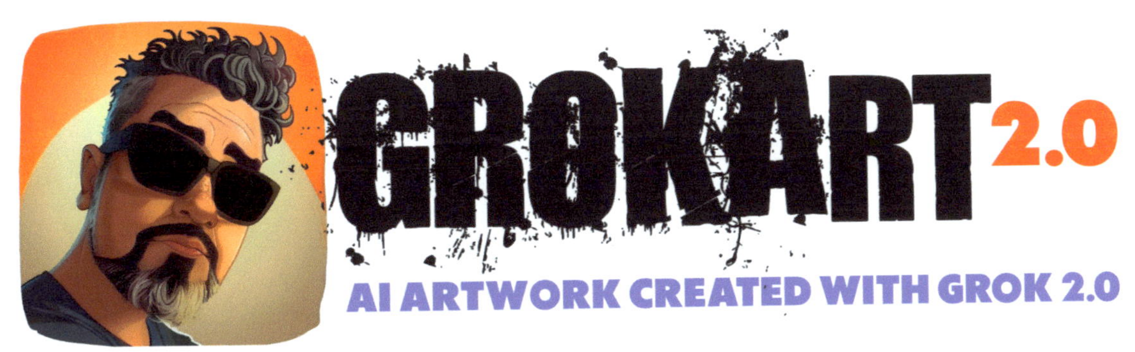

This is BOOK 2 of my series, *The Dreamscape of Ai Art*. The first book didn't come out as good as I wanted it to. So BOOK 2 includes nearly all of the art from BOOK 1.

This book is a collection of Ai artwork, created by me, through GrokAi 2.0. I've always been a creative person and words are the most effective tool I have.

Using words to create digital art may not seem like real art, but in my mind, it is.

I hope you enjoy this second book and I am looking to have a third book and perhaps a fourth book in this series. Thank you so much for all the support my followers have given me.
If you're not following me on X, Rumble, MeWe, YouTube, and TECHAERIS.COM.
Please consider following.

Thanks for purchasing *GROKArt 2.0*, I hope it brings you some joy.

Alex Hernandez

FOR Lisa, Alexandria, Isabel, Ezra, Emilia, and Iliana.
I love you…

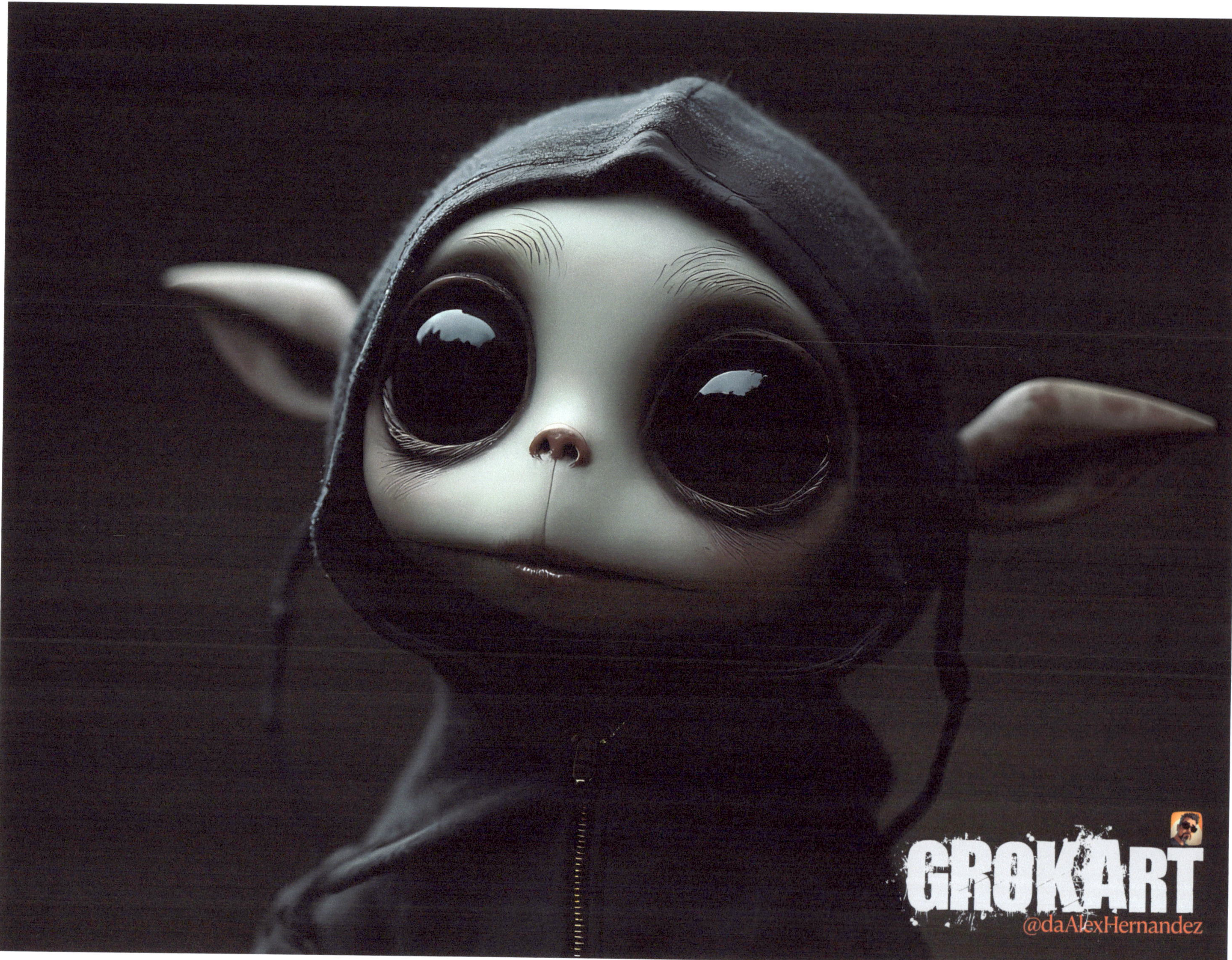
GROKART
@daAlexHernandez

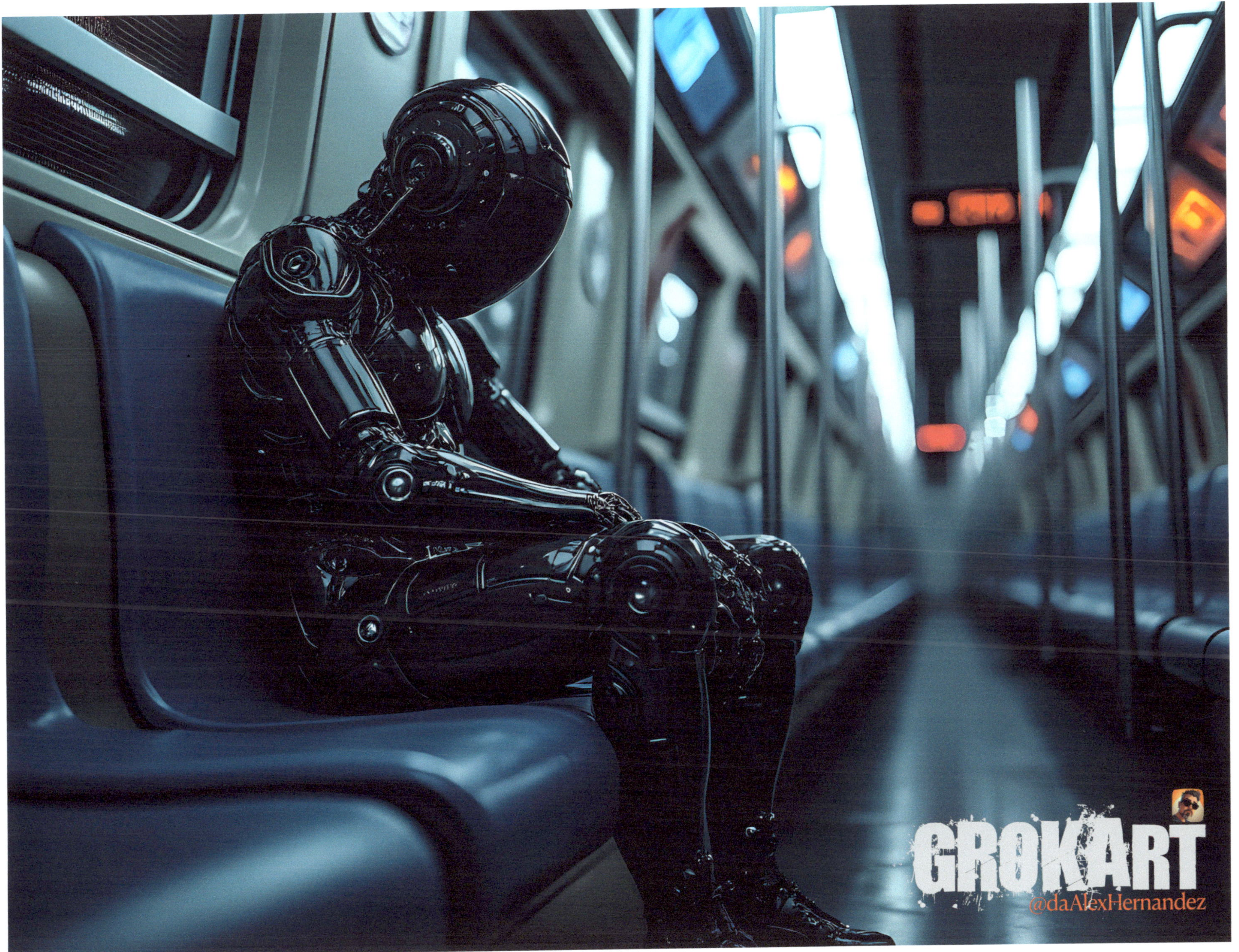
GROKART
@daAlexHernandez

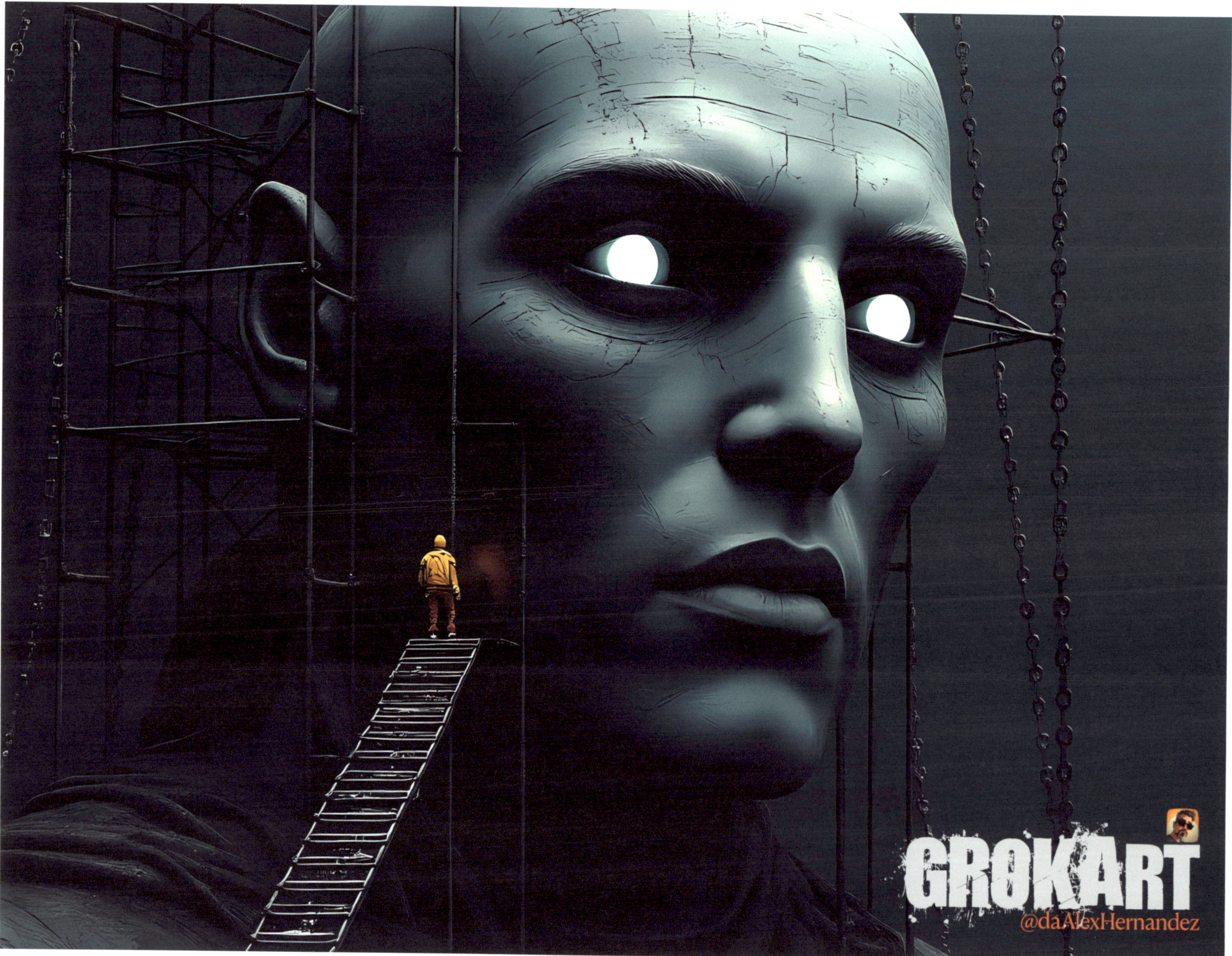

GROKART
@daAlexHernandez

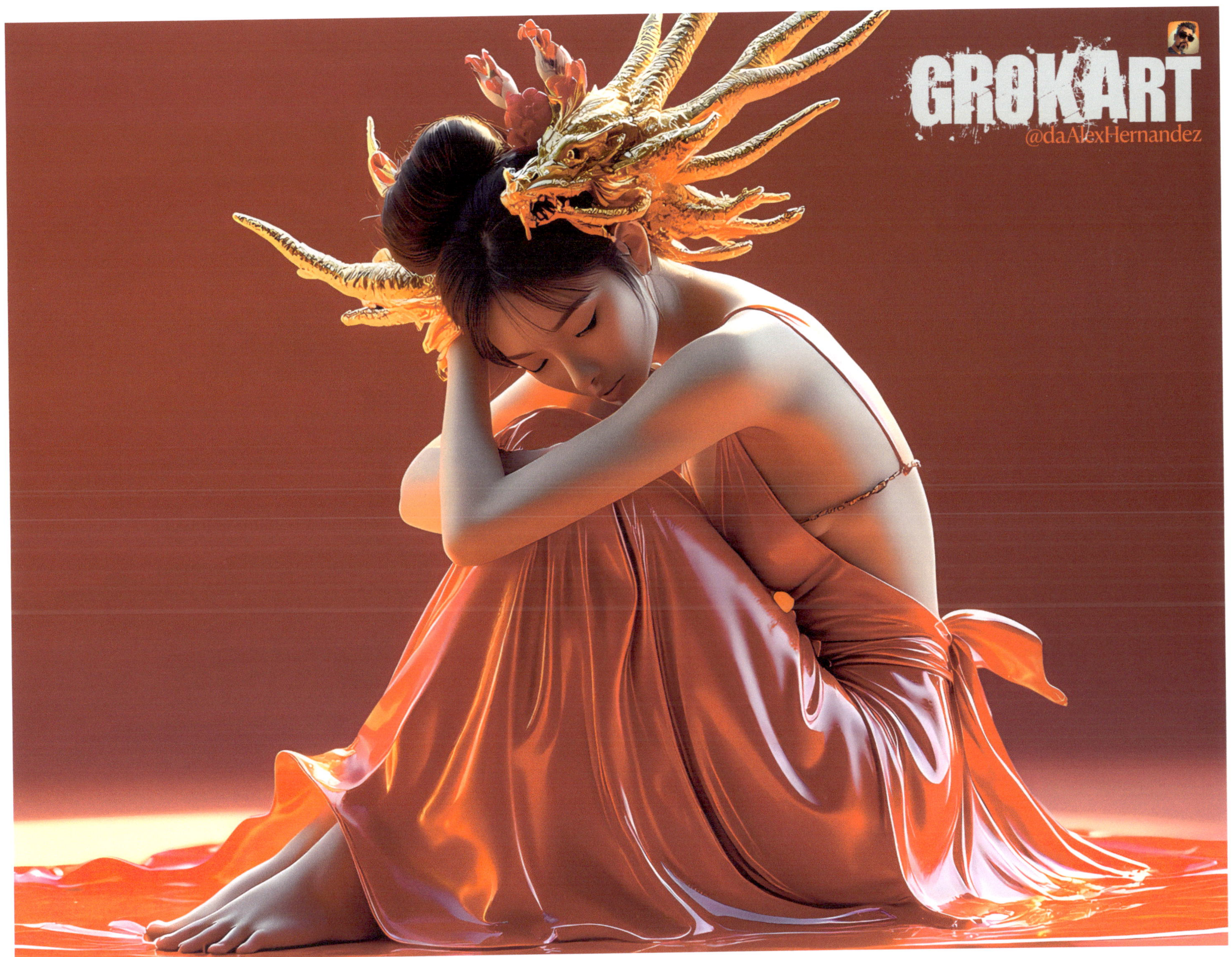

GROKART
@daAlexHernandez

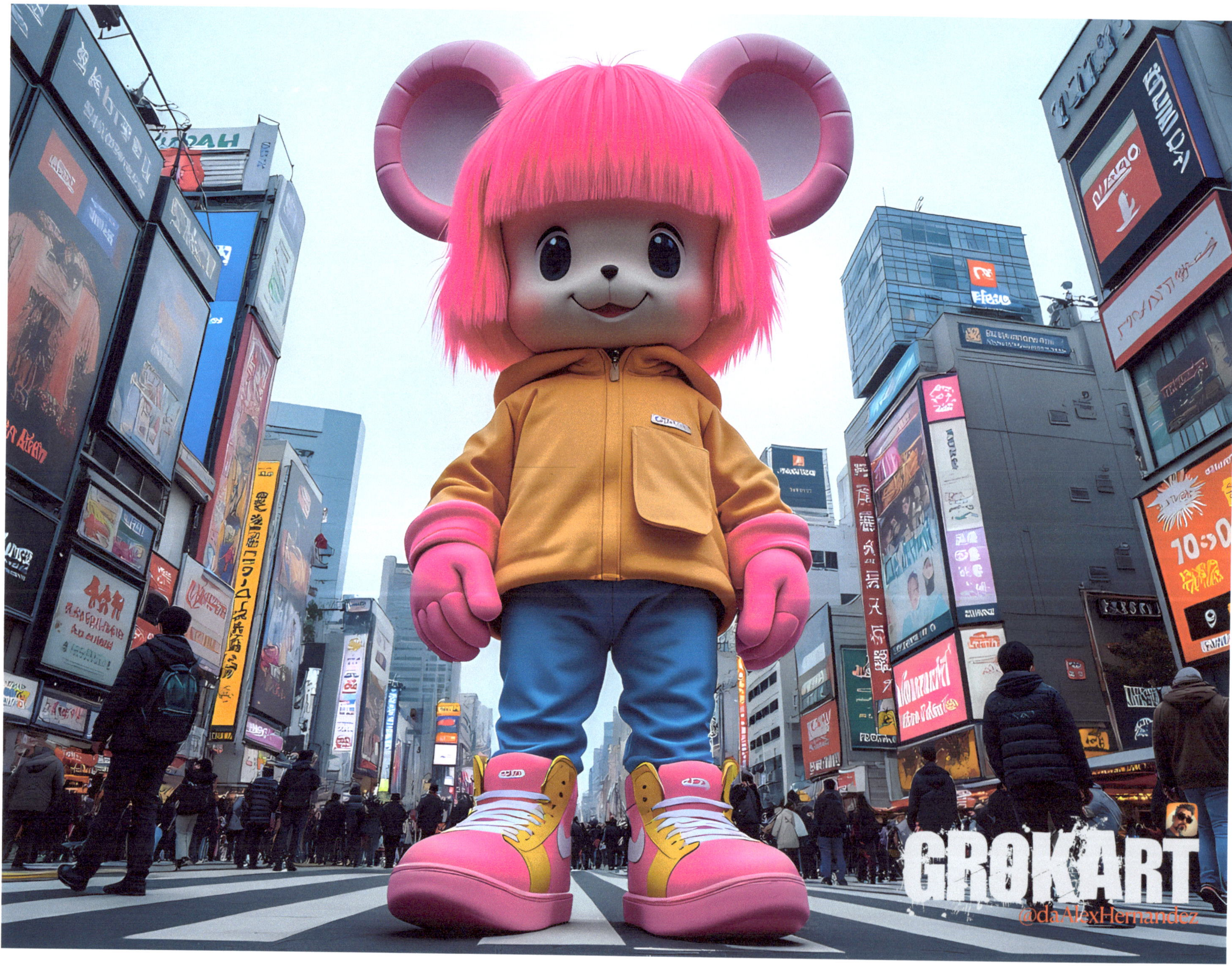

GROKART
@daAlexHernandez

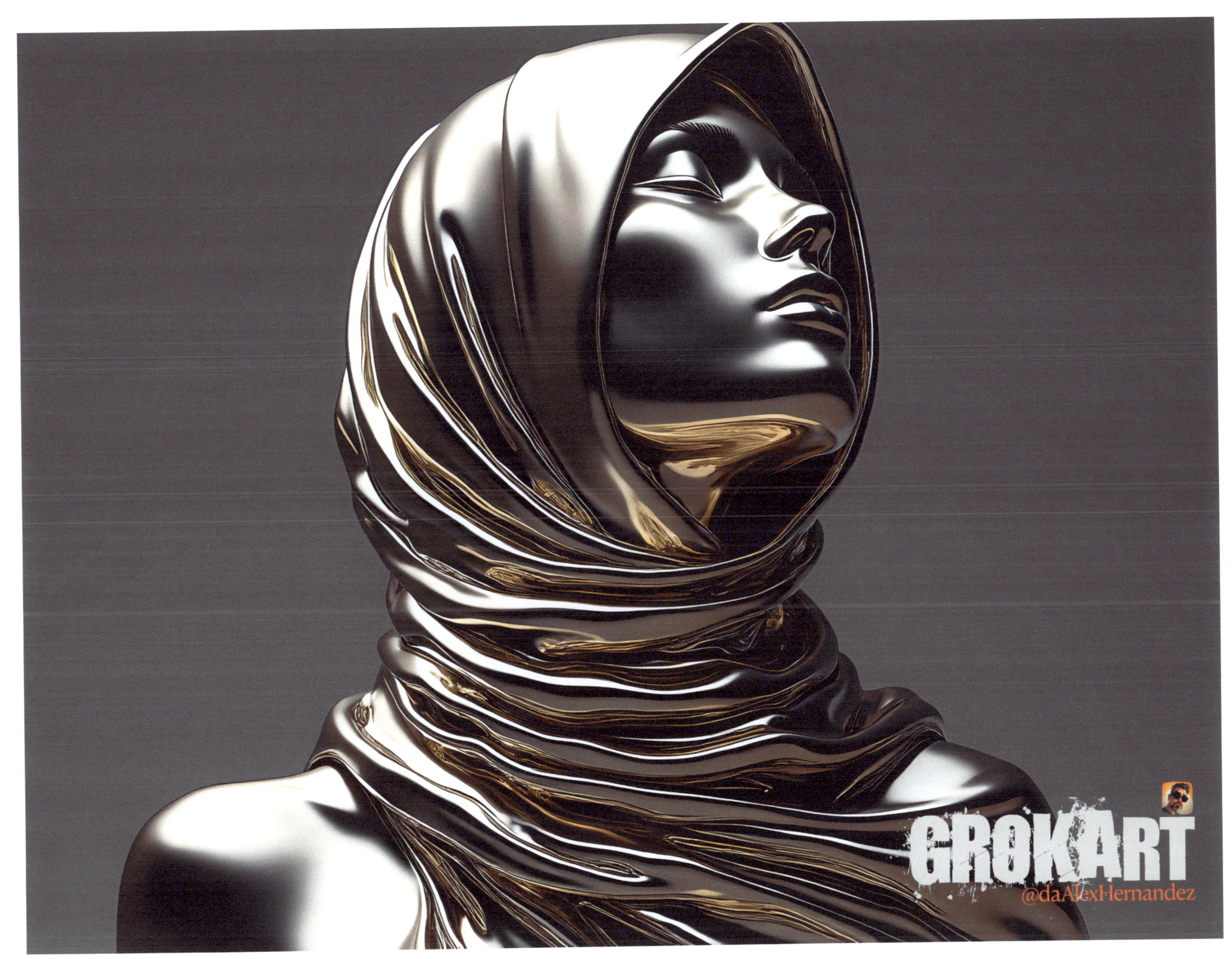
GROKART
@daAlexHernandez

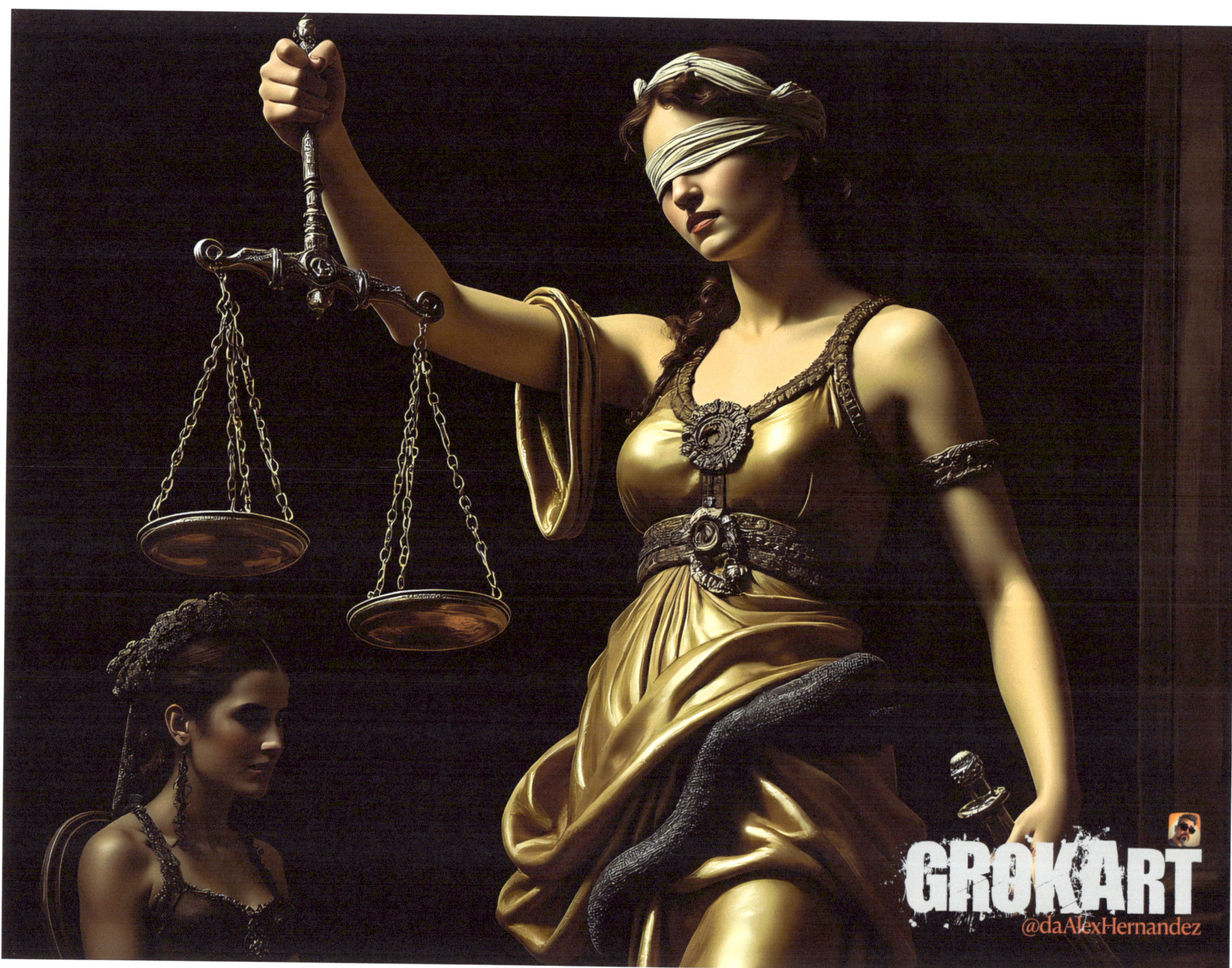

GROKART
@daAlexHernandez

GROKART
@daAlexHernandez

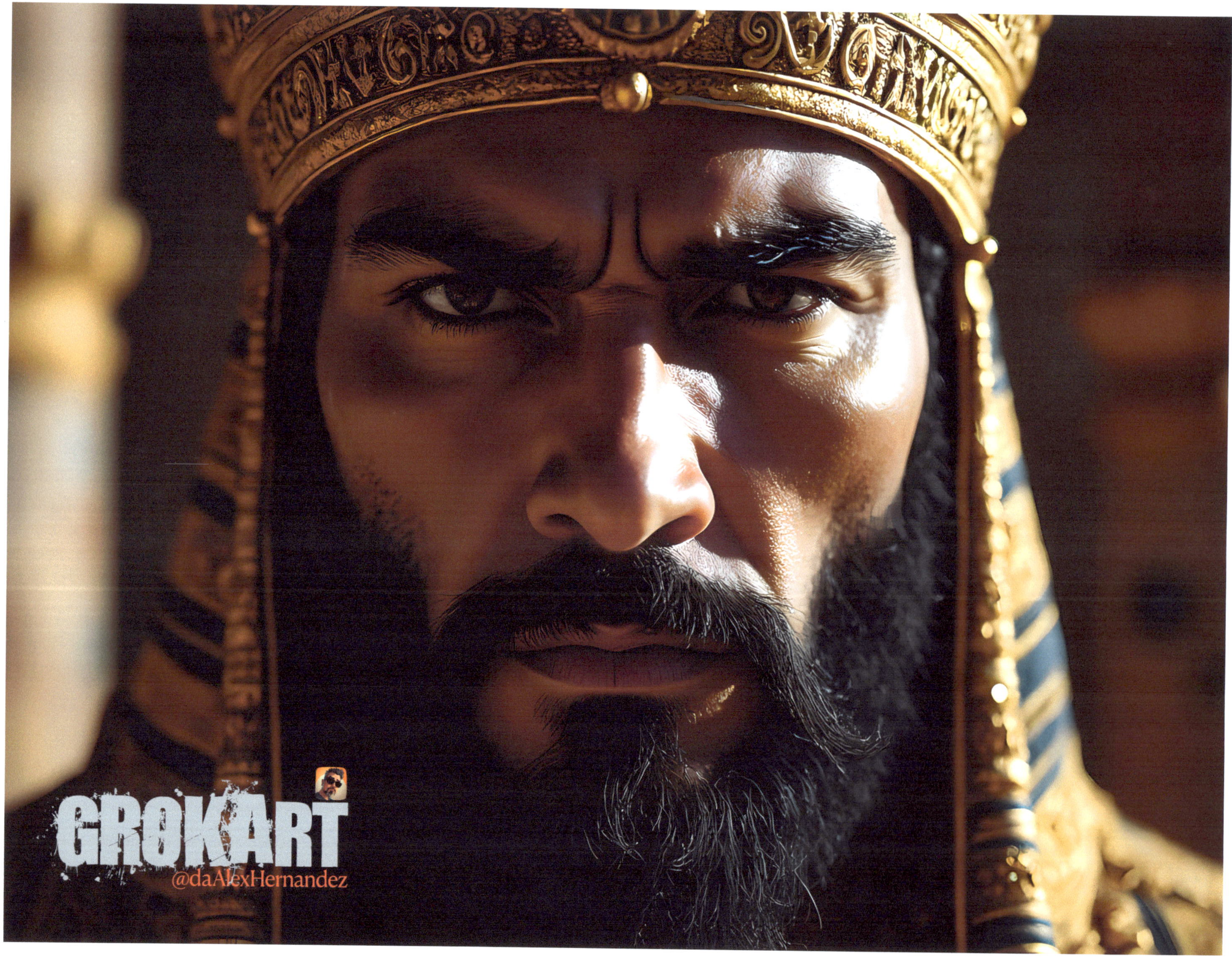
GROKART
@daAlexHernandez

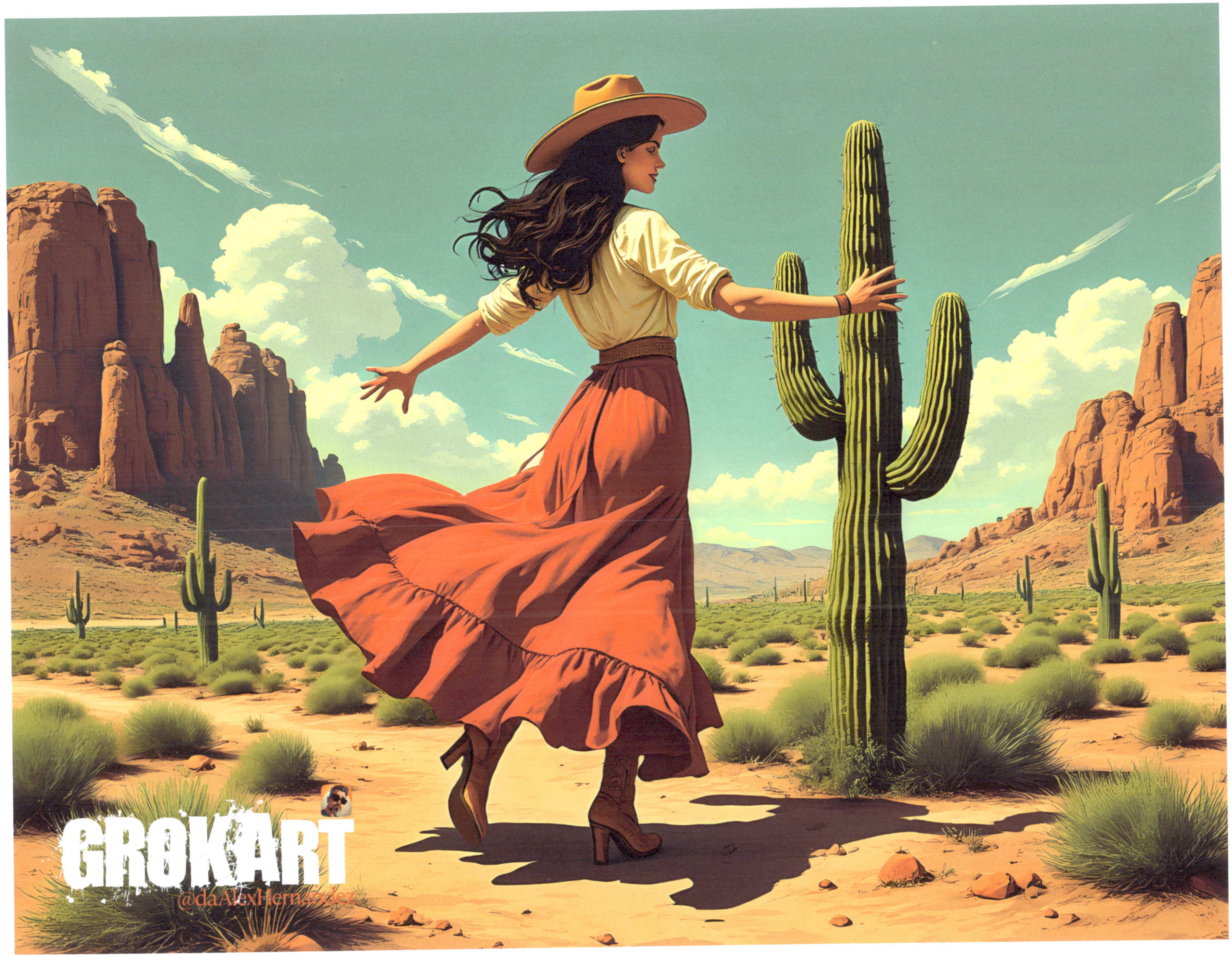

GROKART
@daAlexHernandez

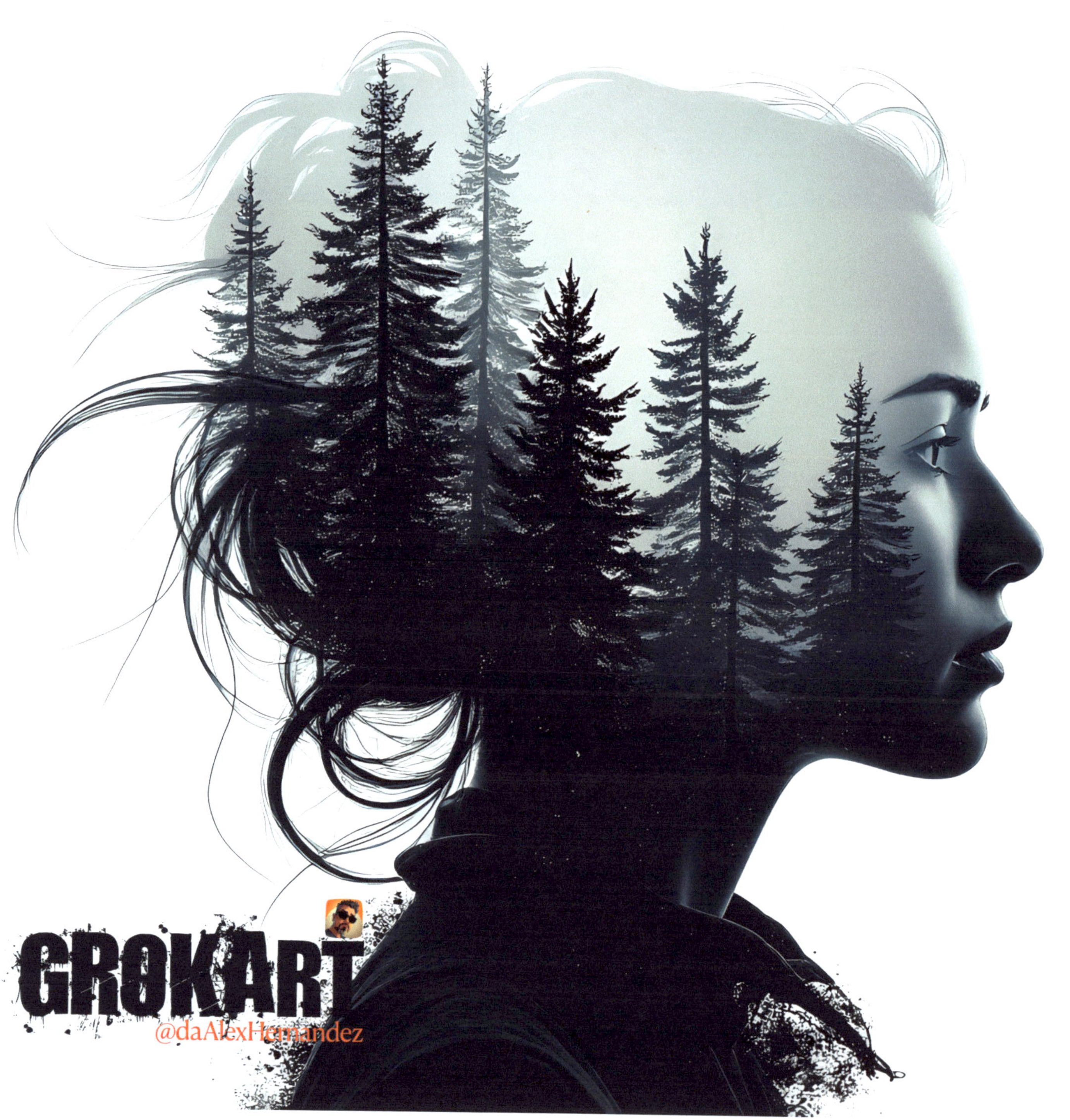

GROKART
@daAlexHernandez

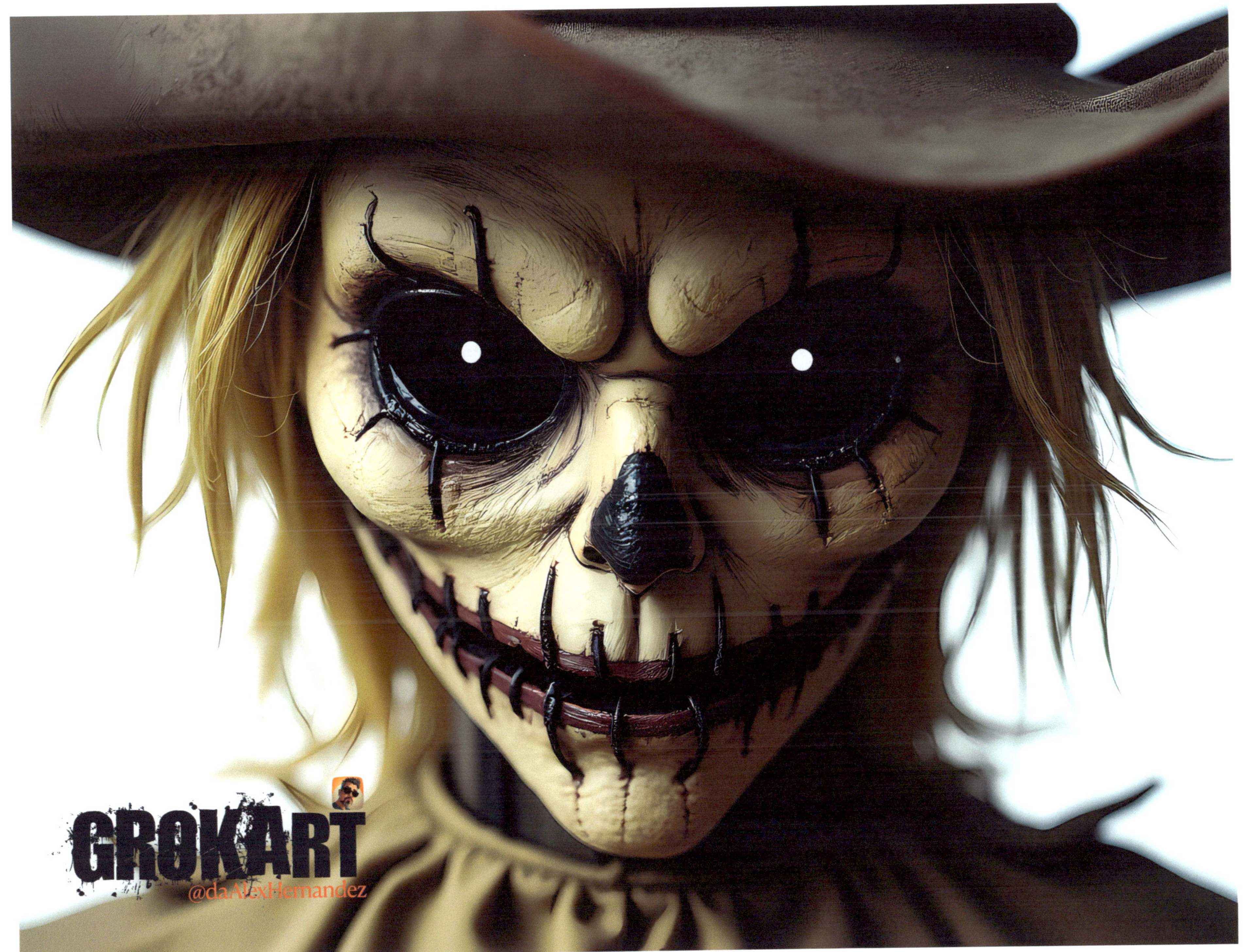

GROKART
@daAlexHernandez

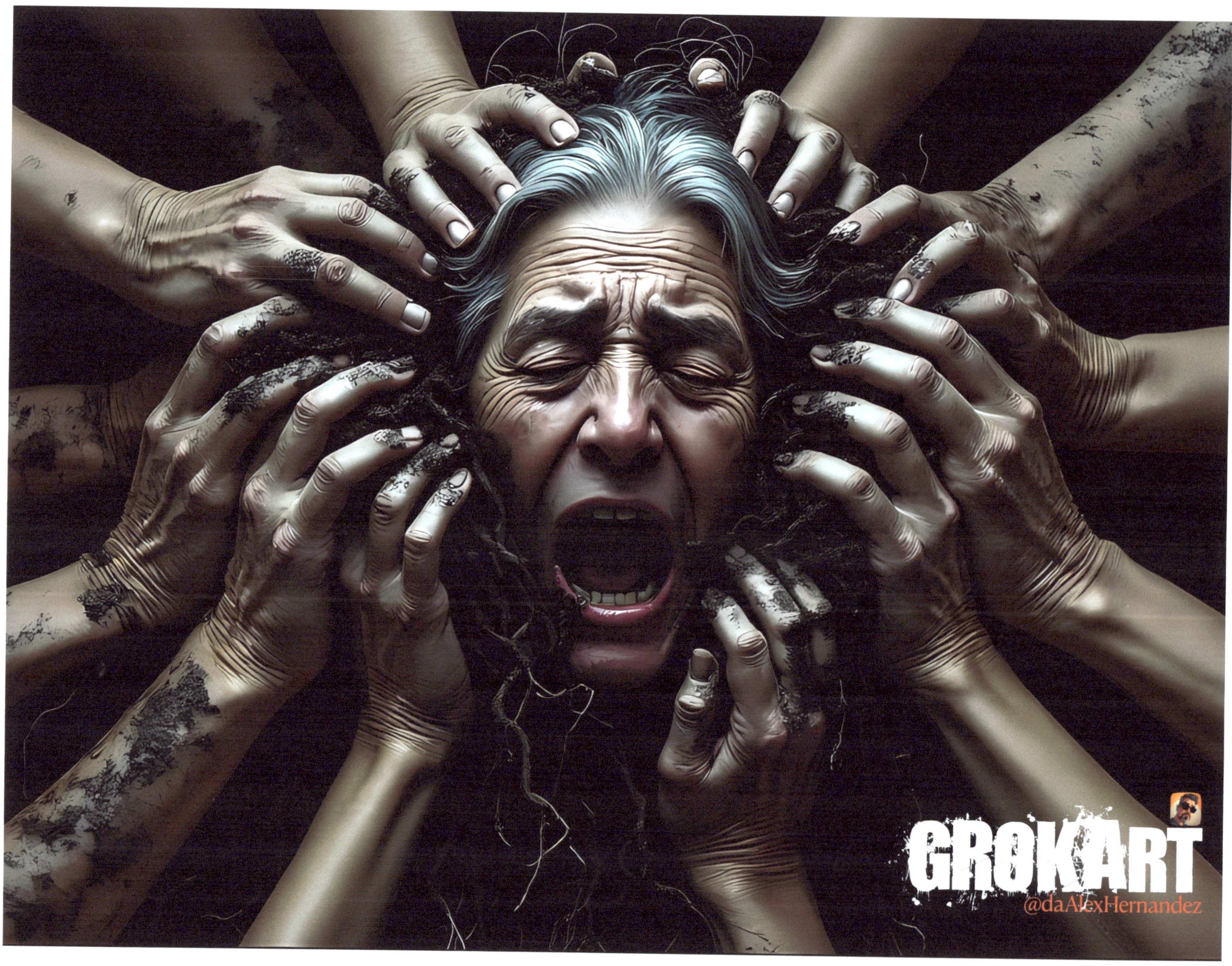
GROKART
@daAlexHernandez

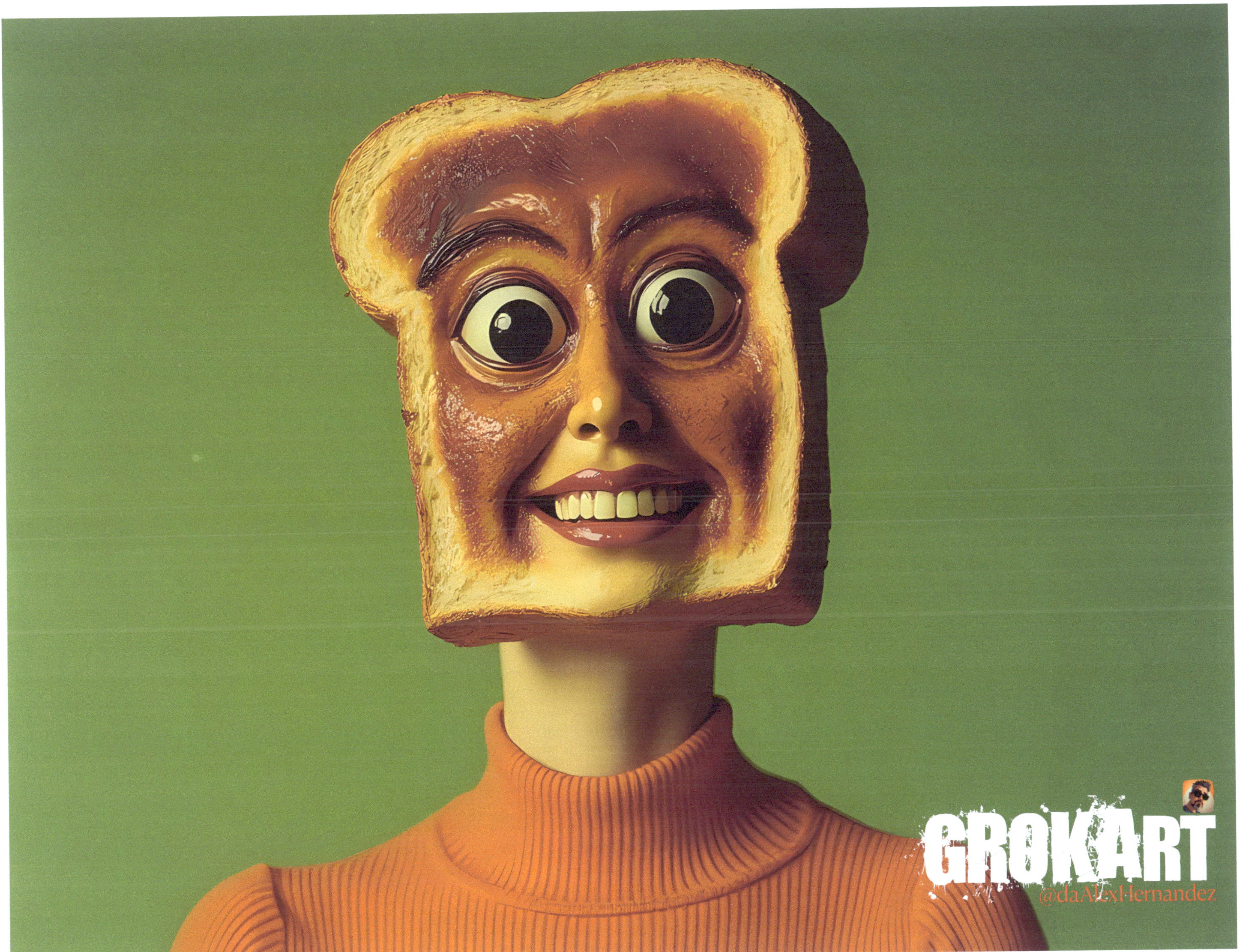
GROKART
@daAlexHernandez

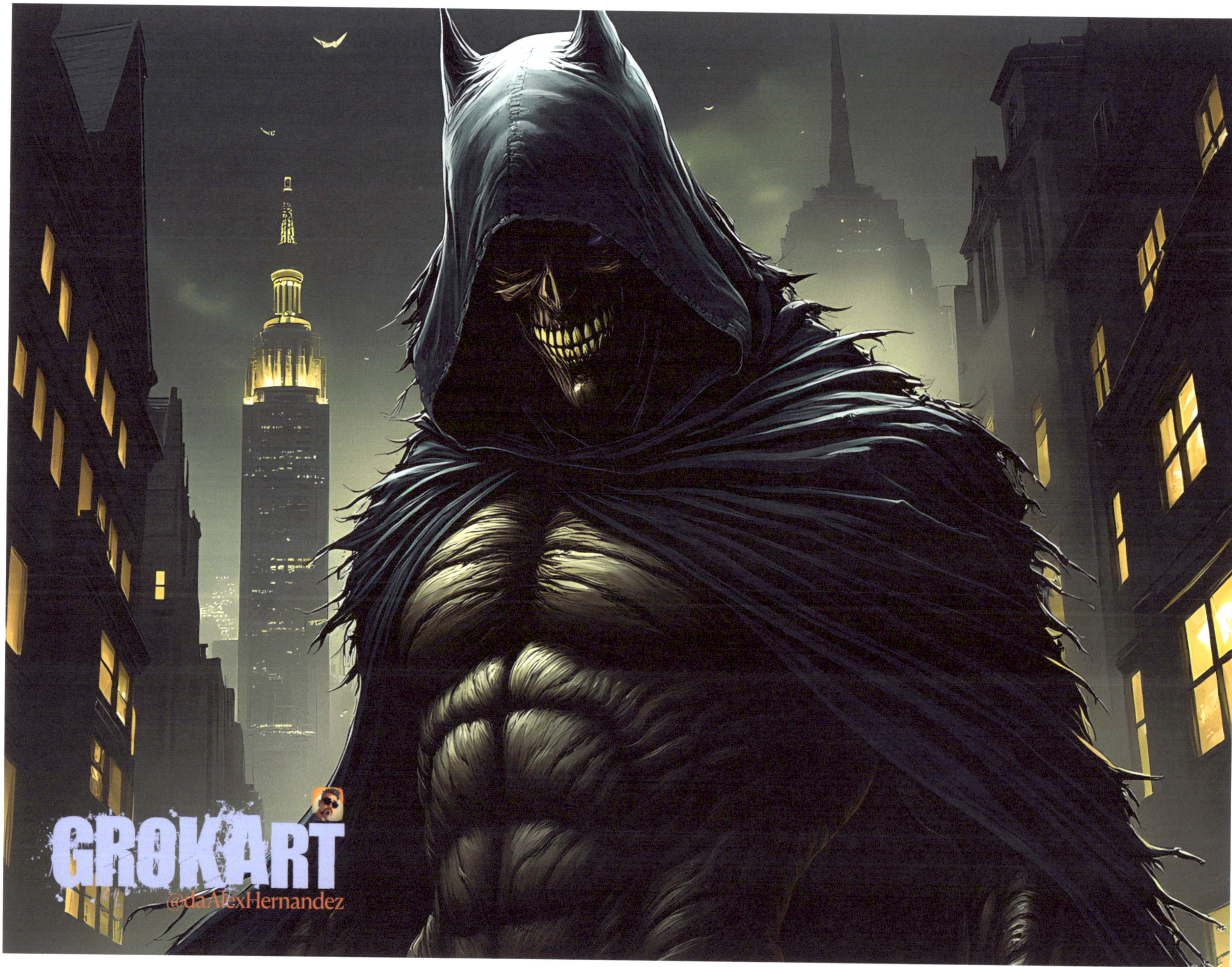
GROKART
@daAlexHernandez

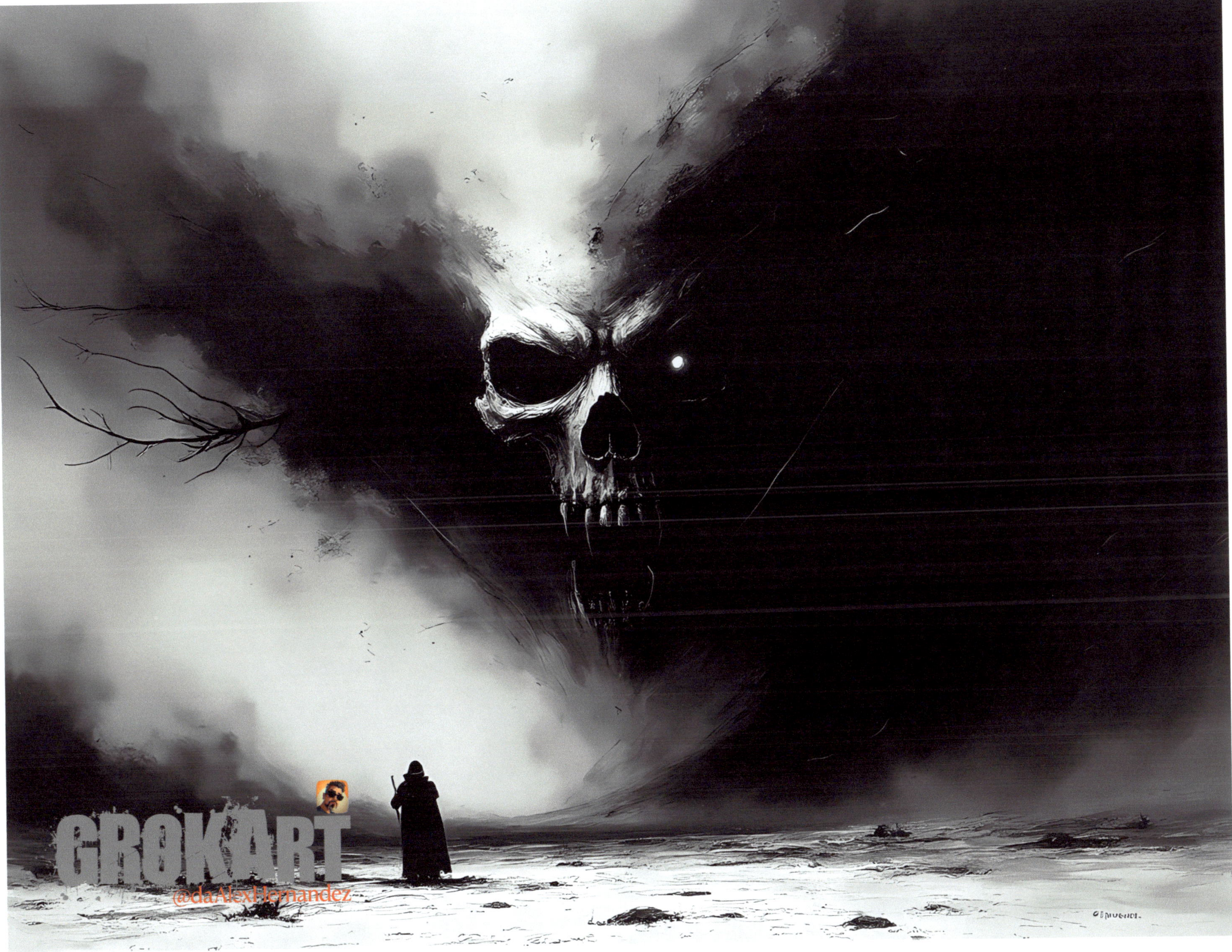

GROKART
@daAlexHernandez

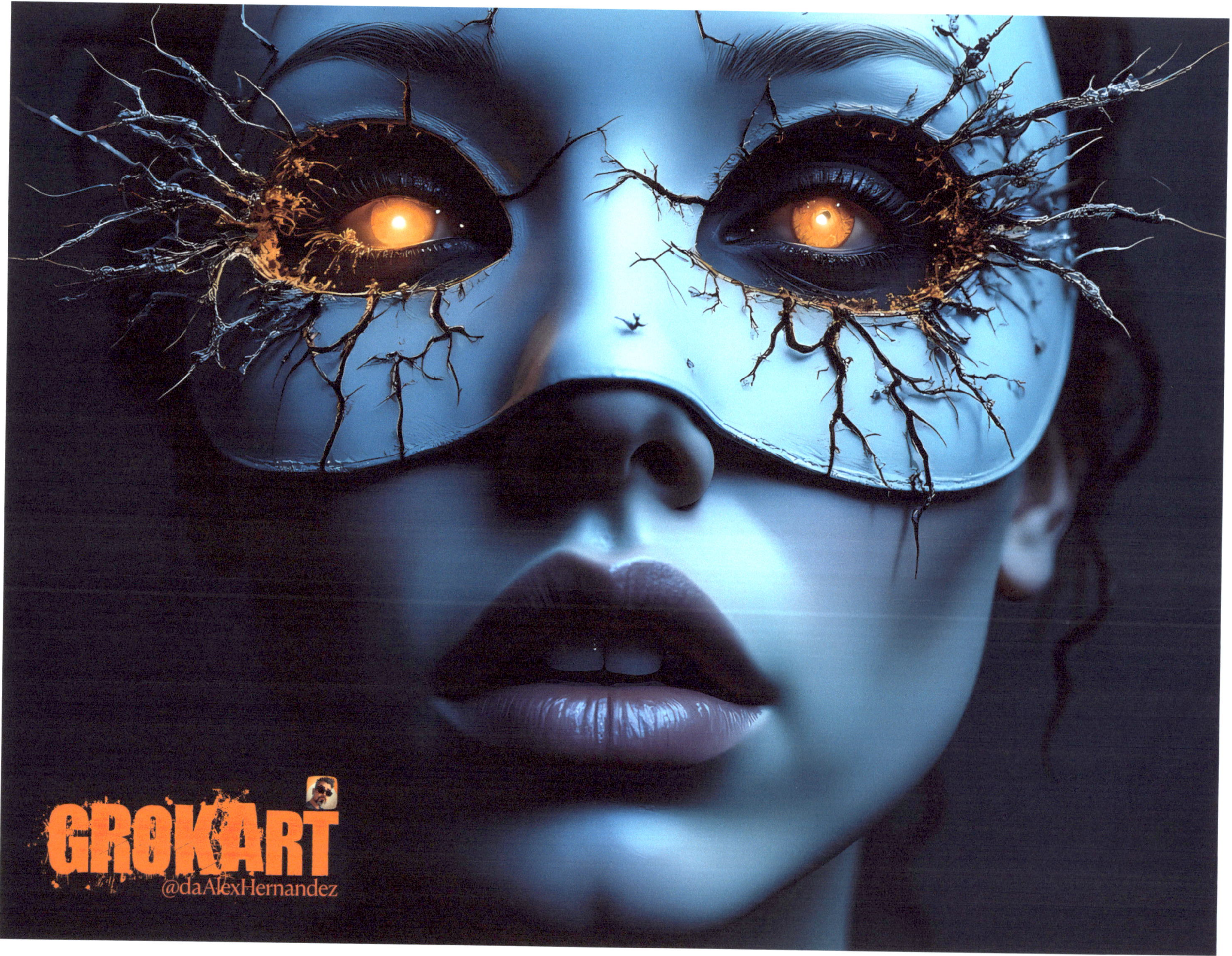
GROKART
@daAlexHernandez

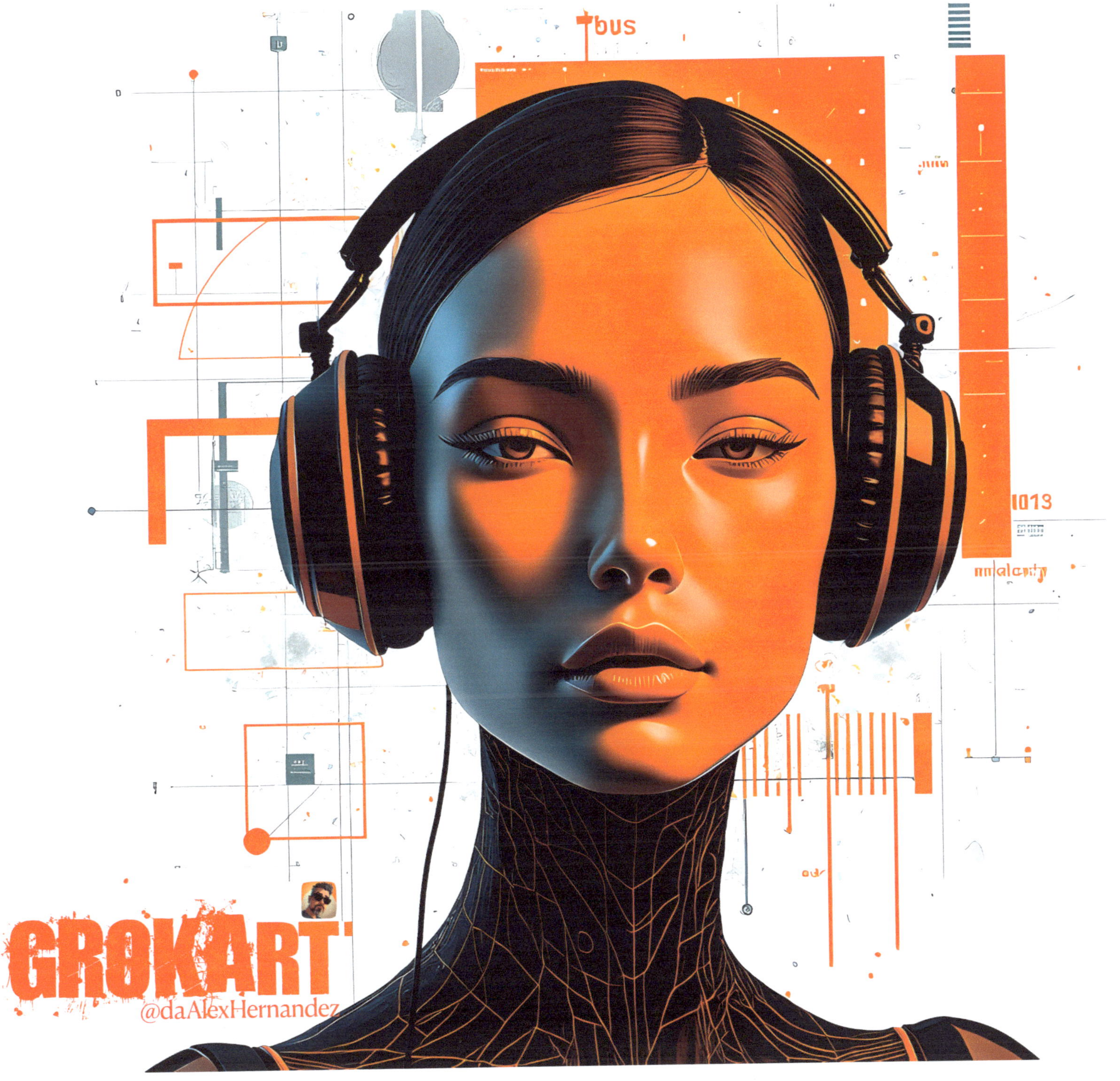
GROKART
@daAlexHernandez

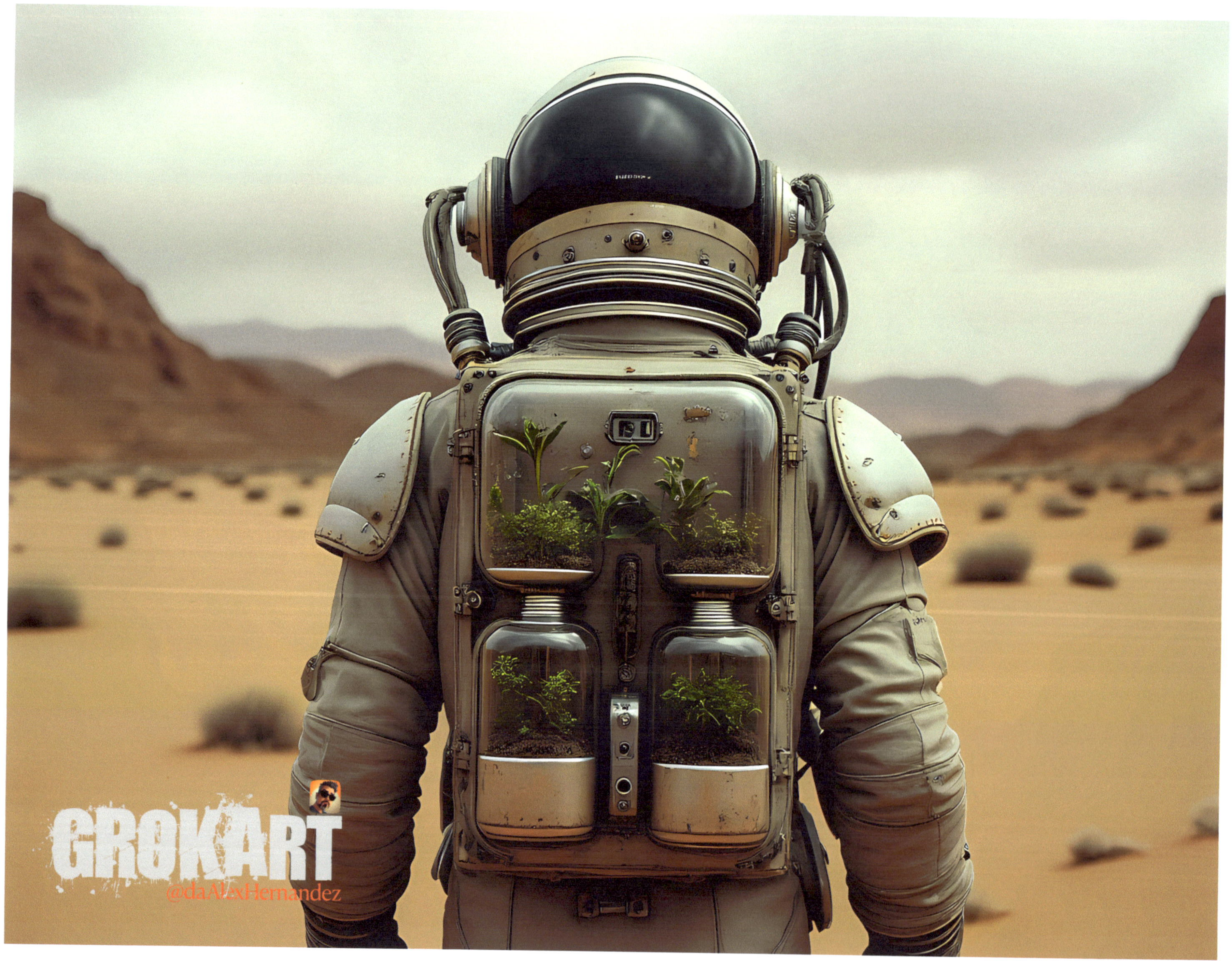
GROKART
@daAlexHernandez

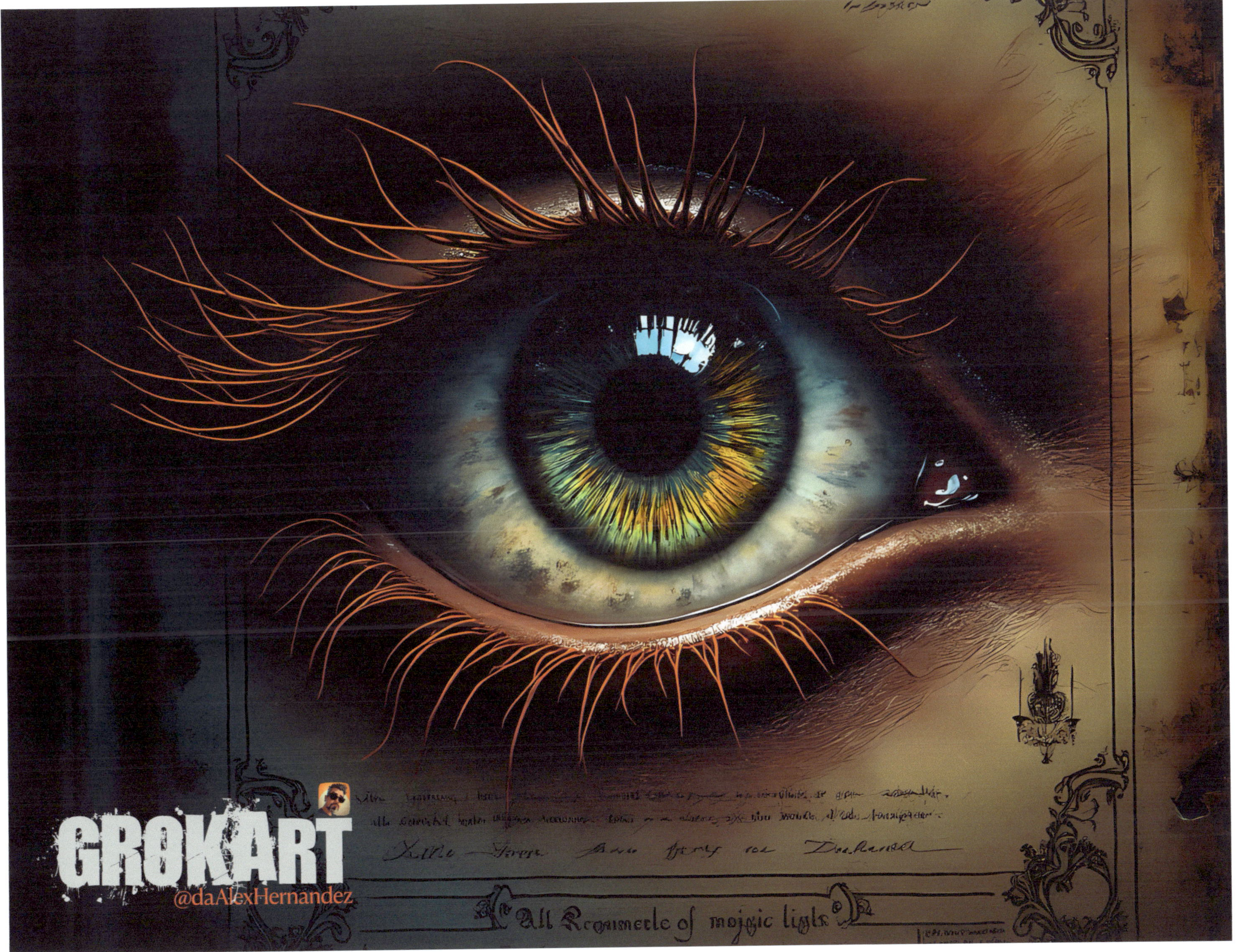

GROKART
@daAlexHernandez
All Rcosmecle of mojgic ligts

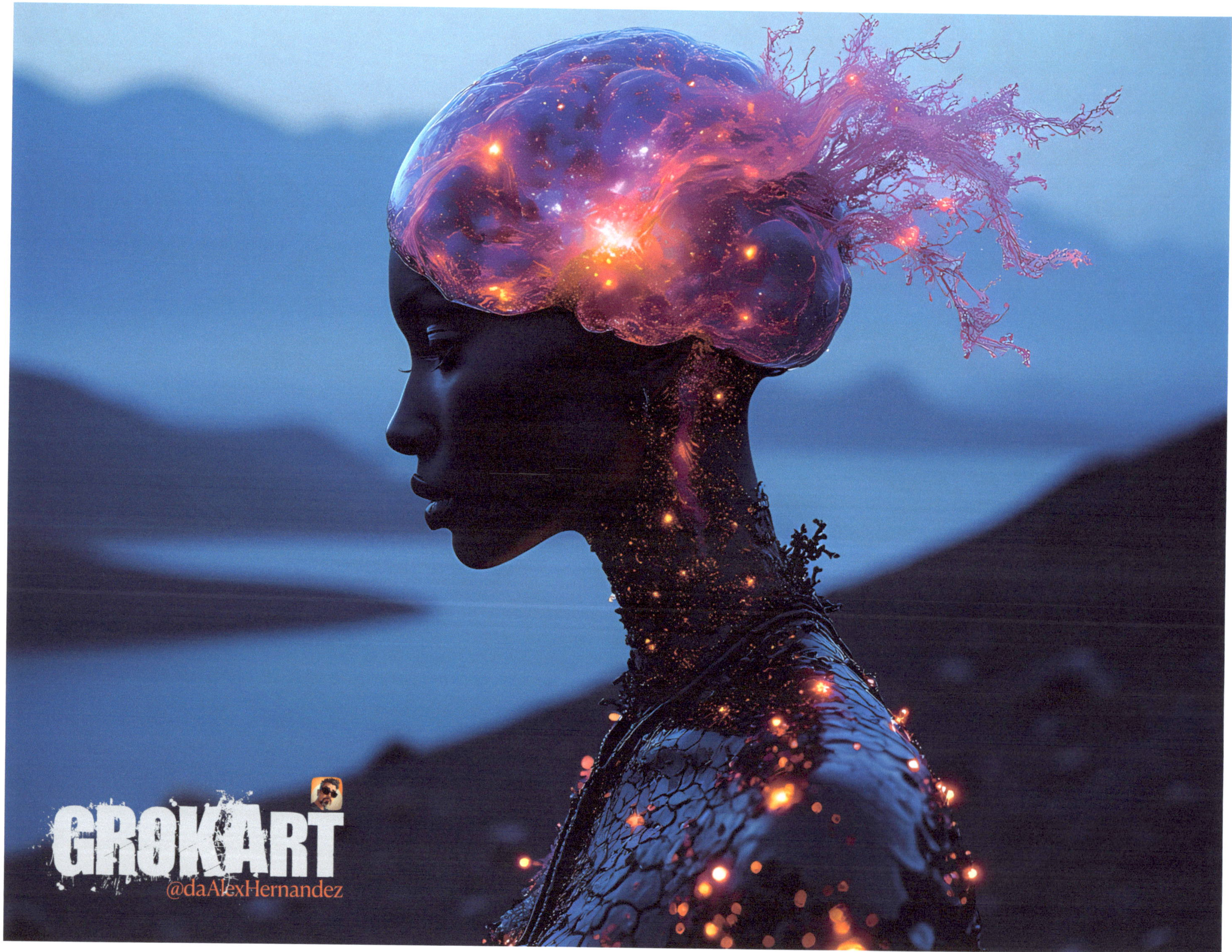

GROKART
@daAlexHernandez

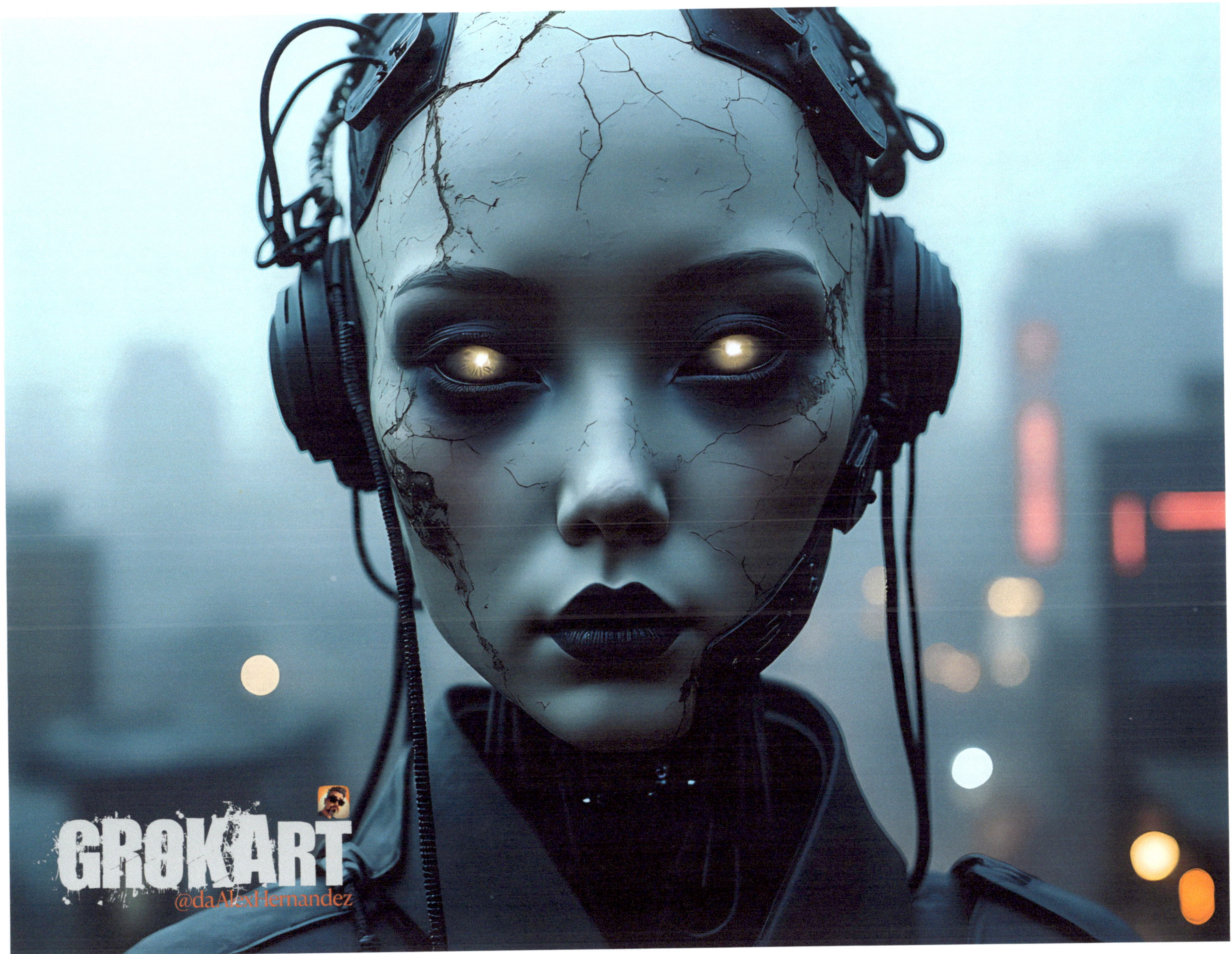
GROKART
@daAlexHernandez

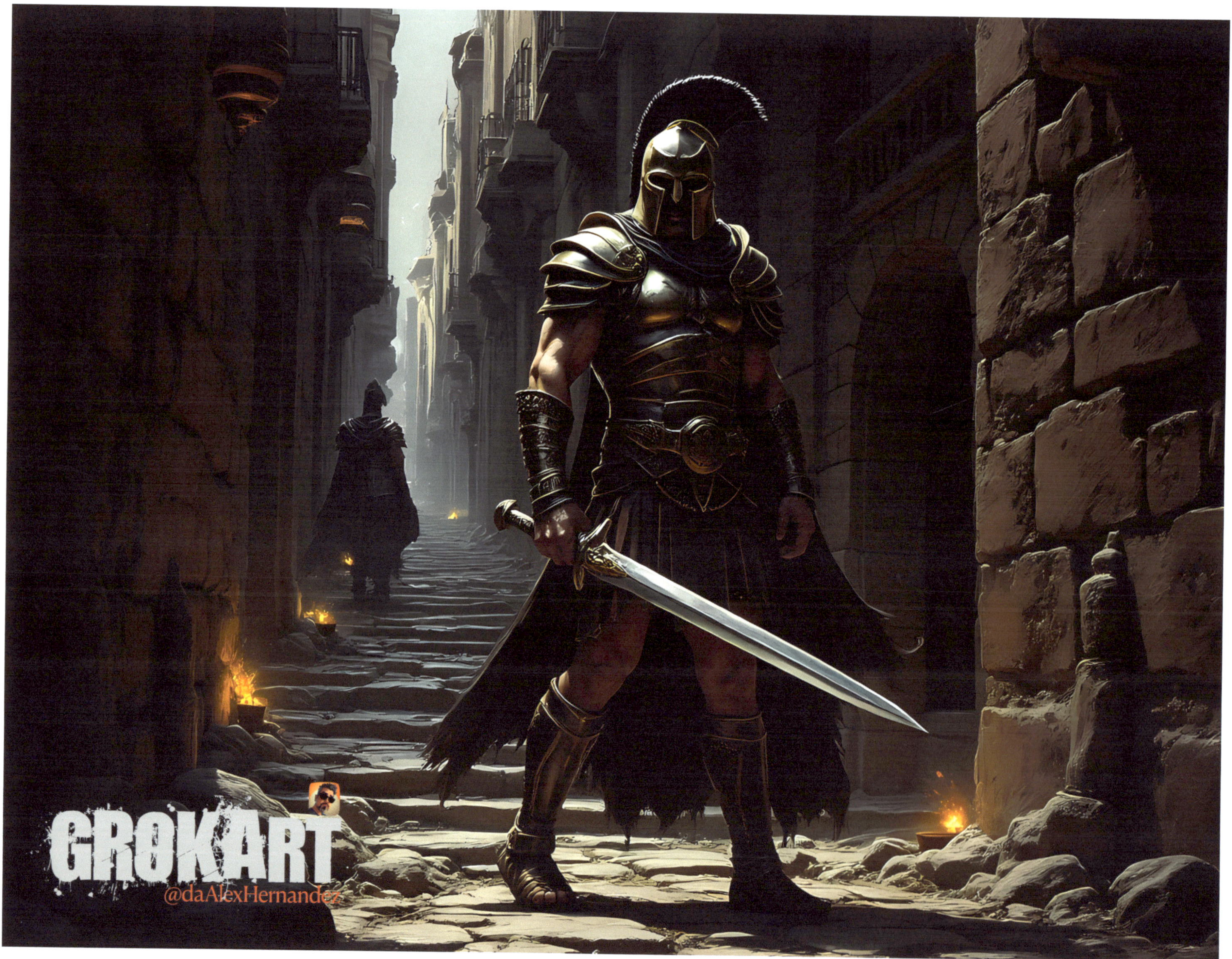
GROKART
@daAlexHernandez

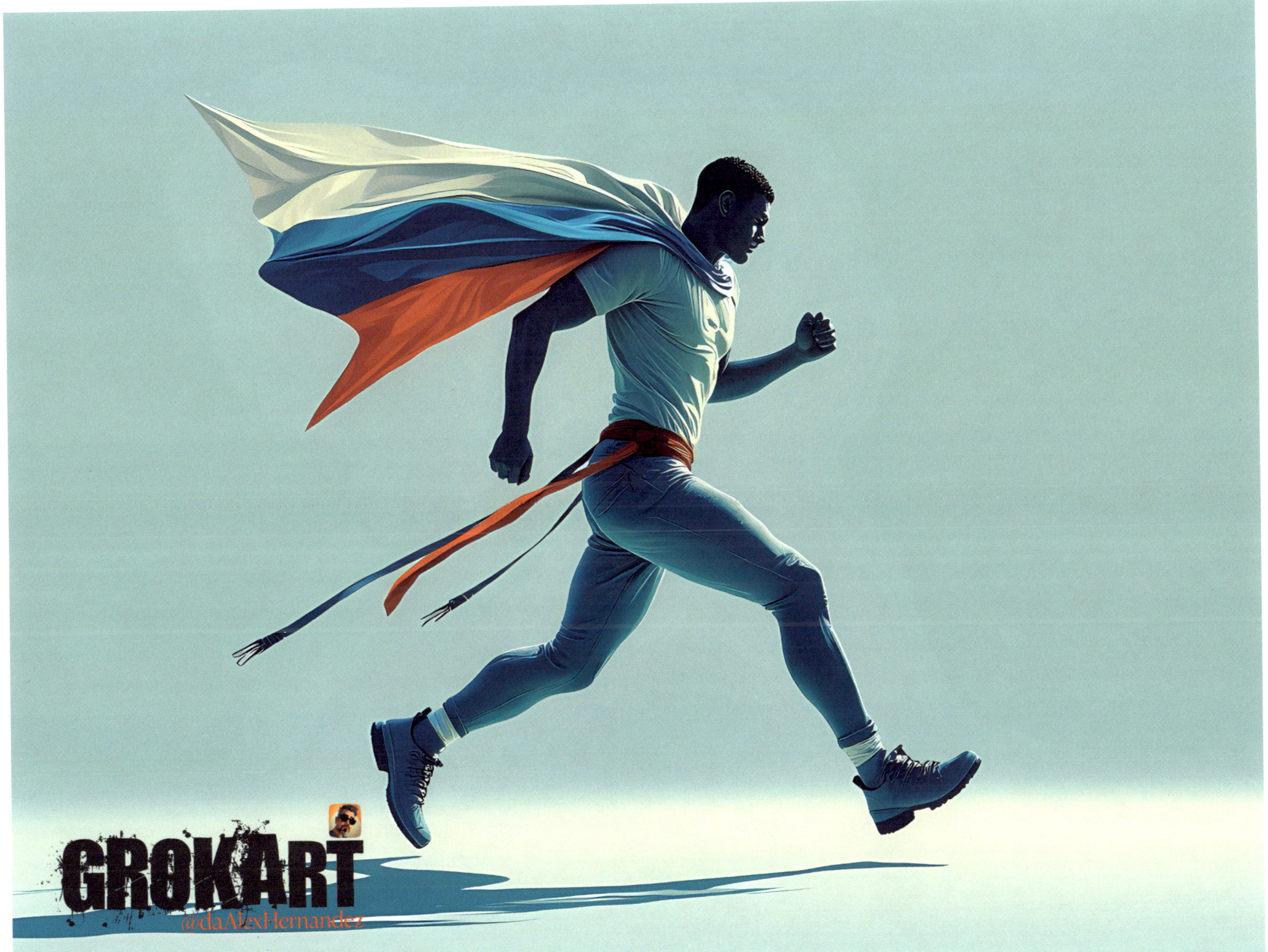

GROKART
@daAlexHernandez

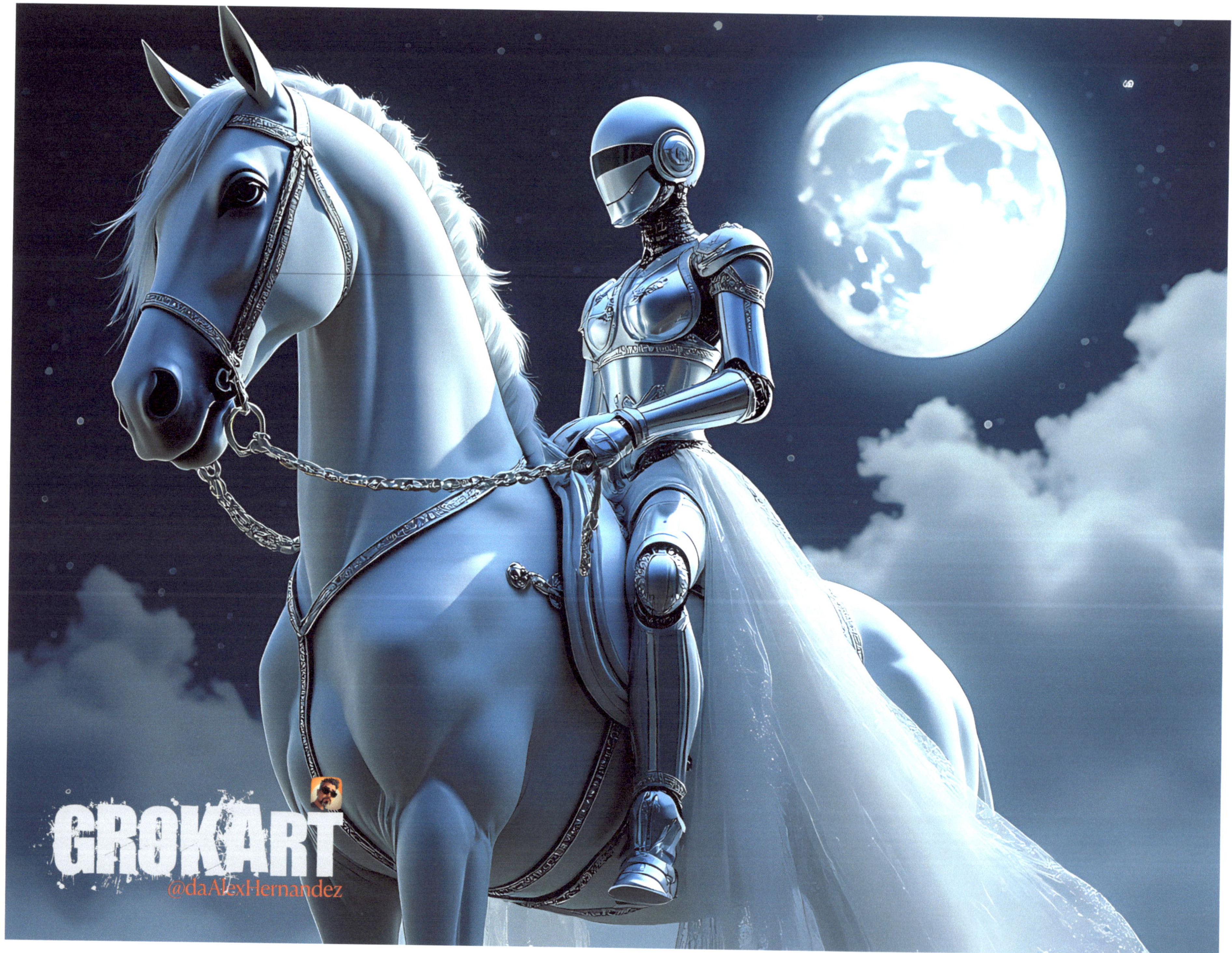
GR0KART
@daAlexHernandez

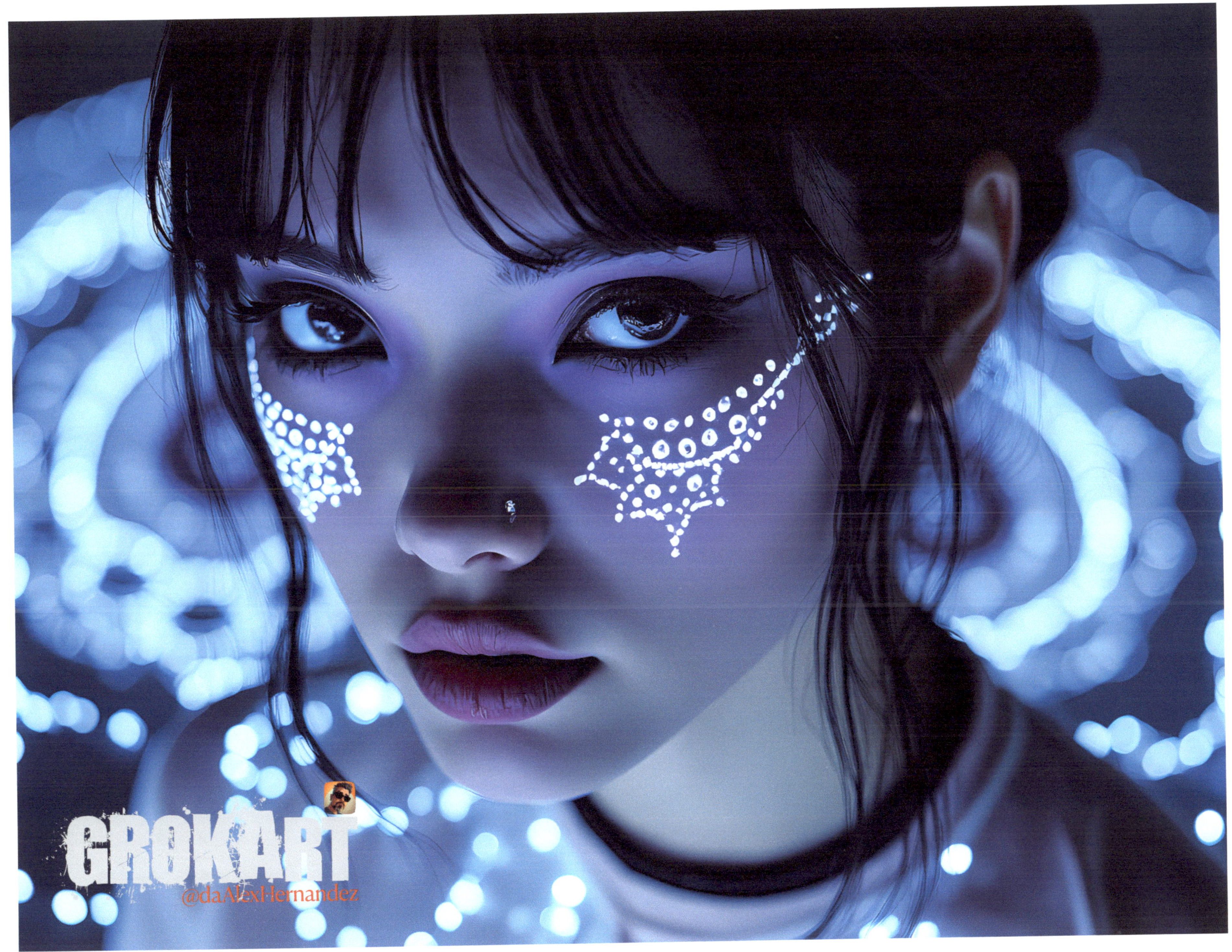

GROKART
@daAlexHernandez

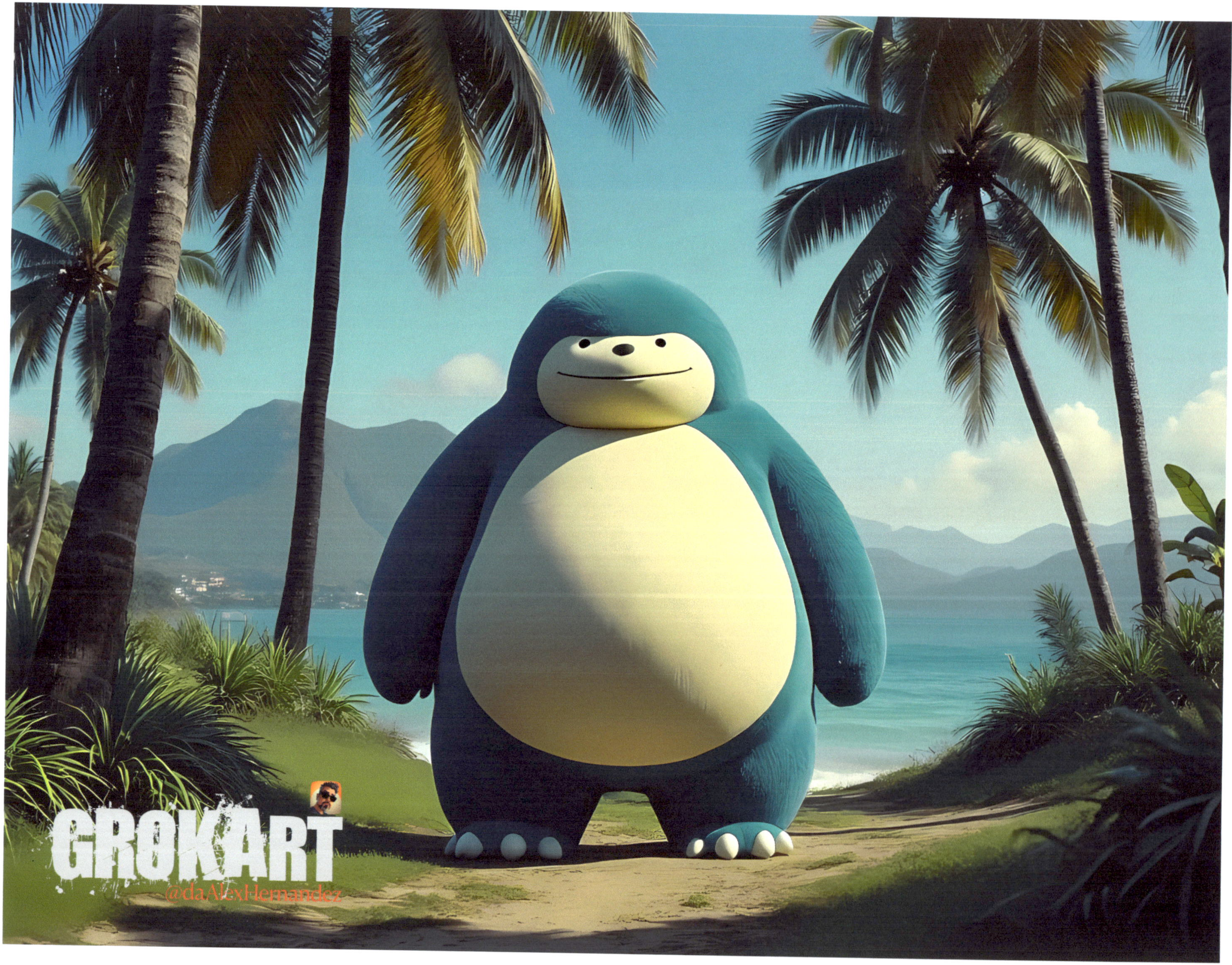
GROKART
@daAlexHernandez

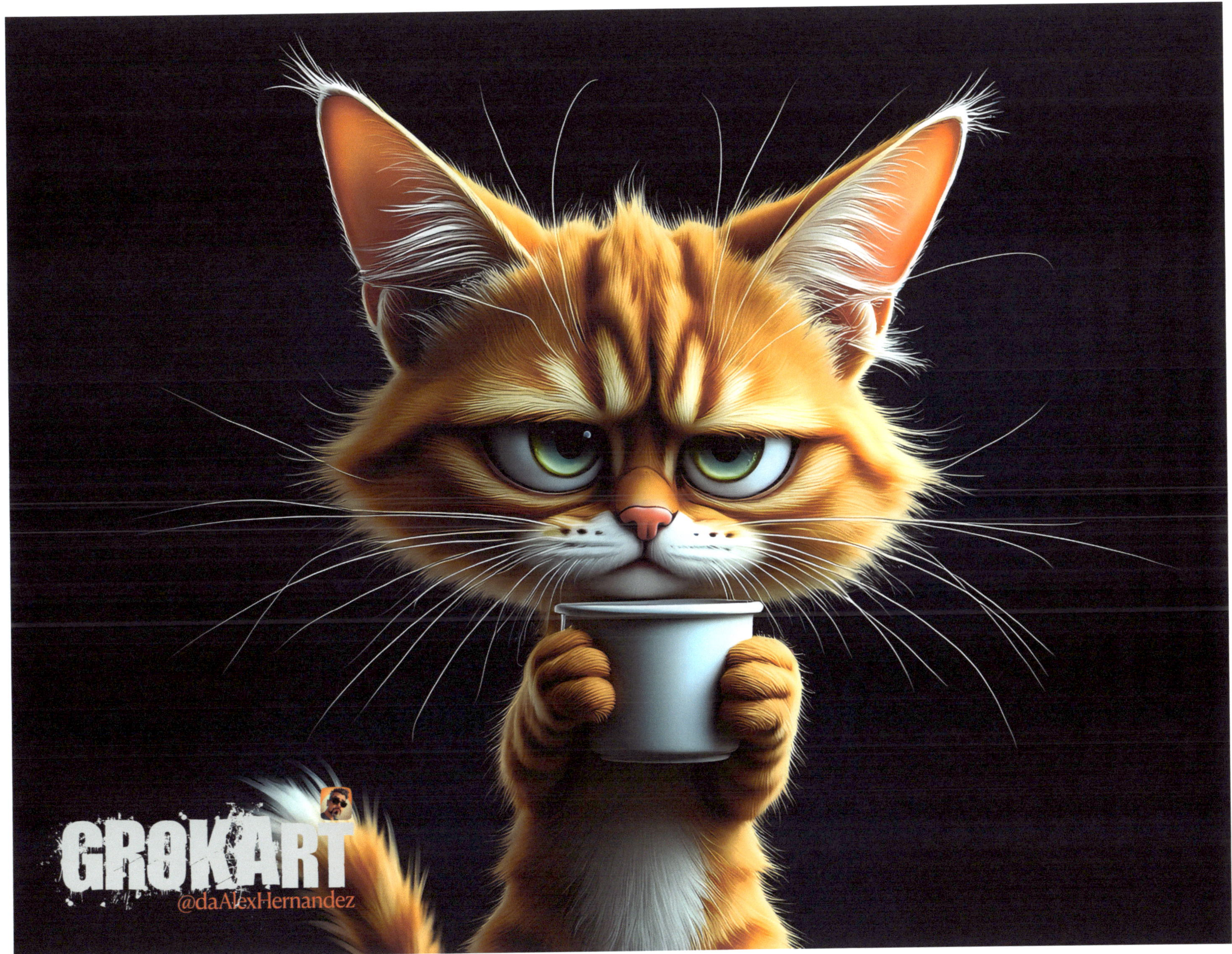
GROKART
@daAlexHernandez

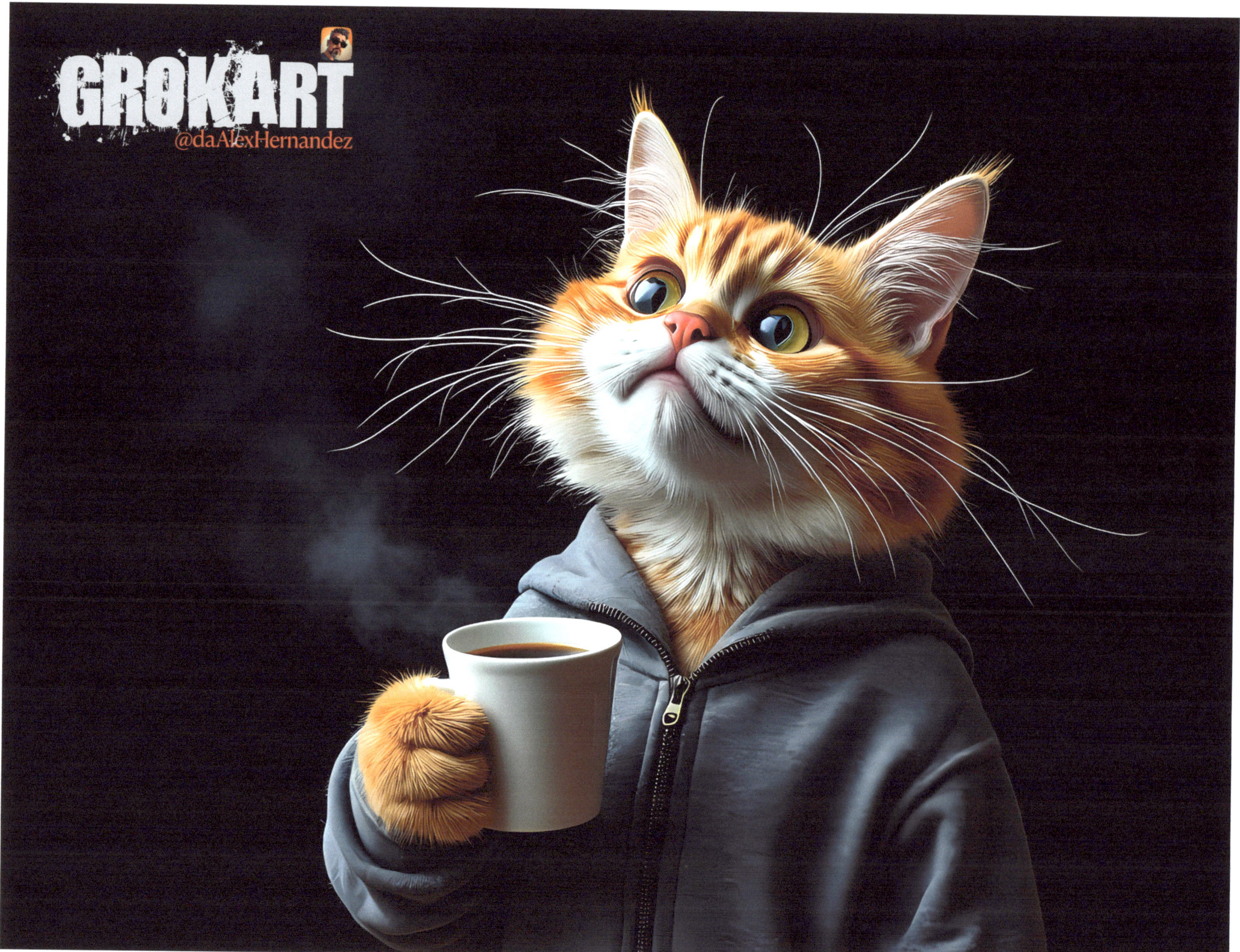

GROKART
@daAlexHernandez

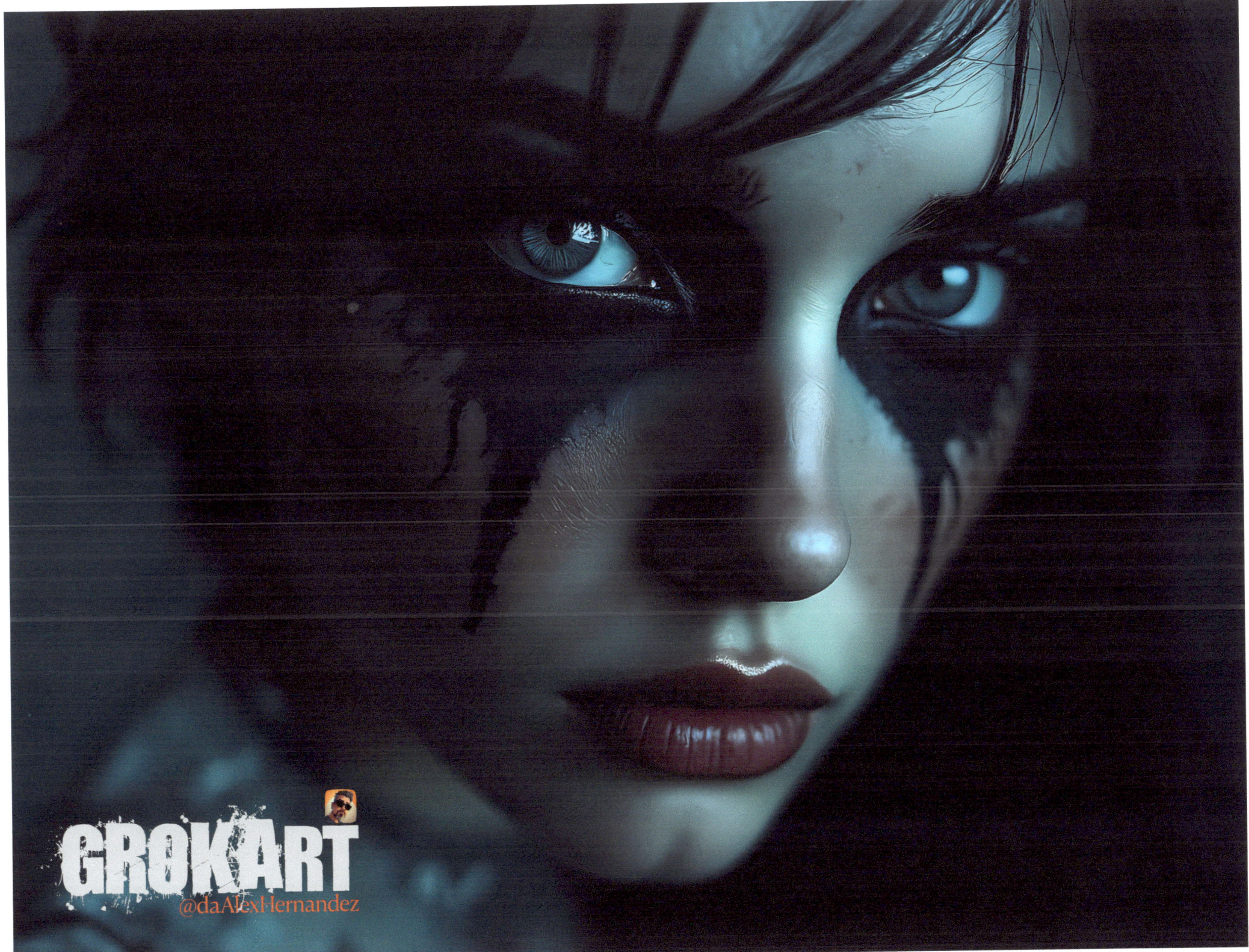

GROKART
@daAlexHernandez

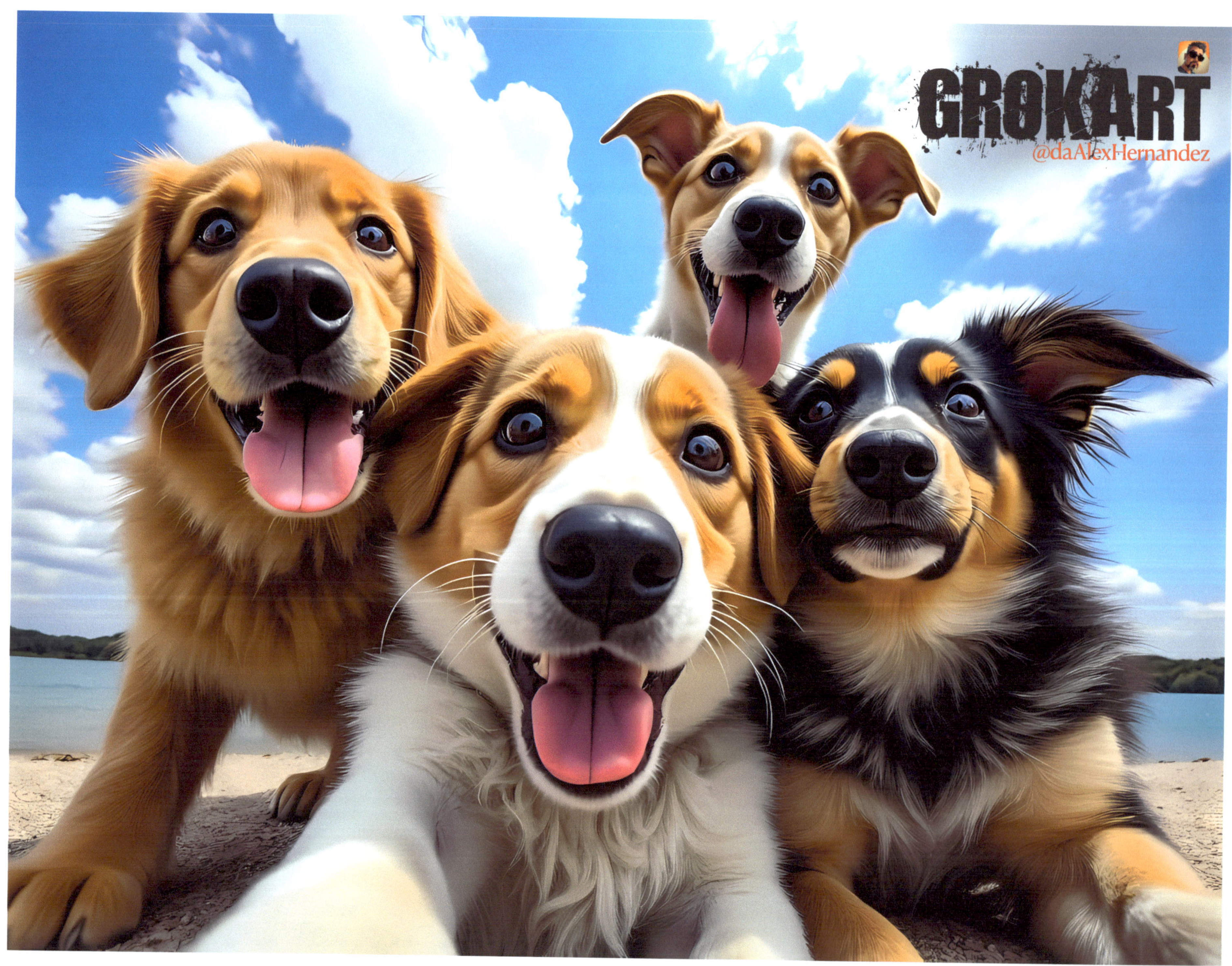

GROKART
@daAlexHernandez

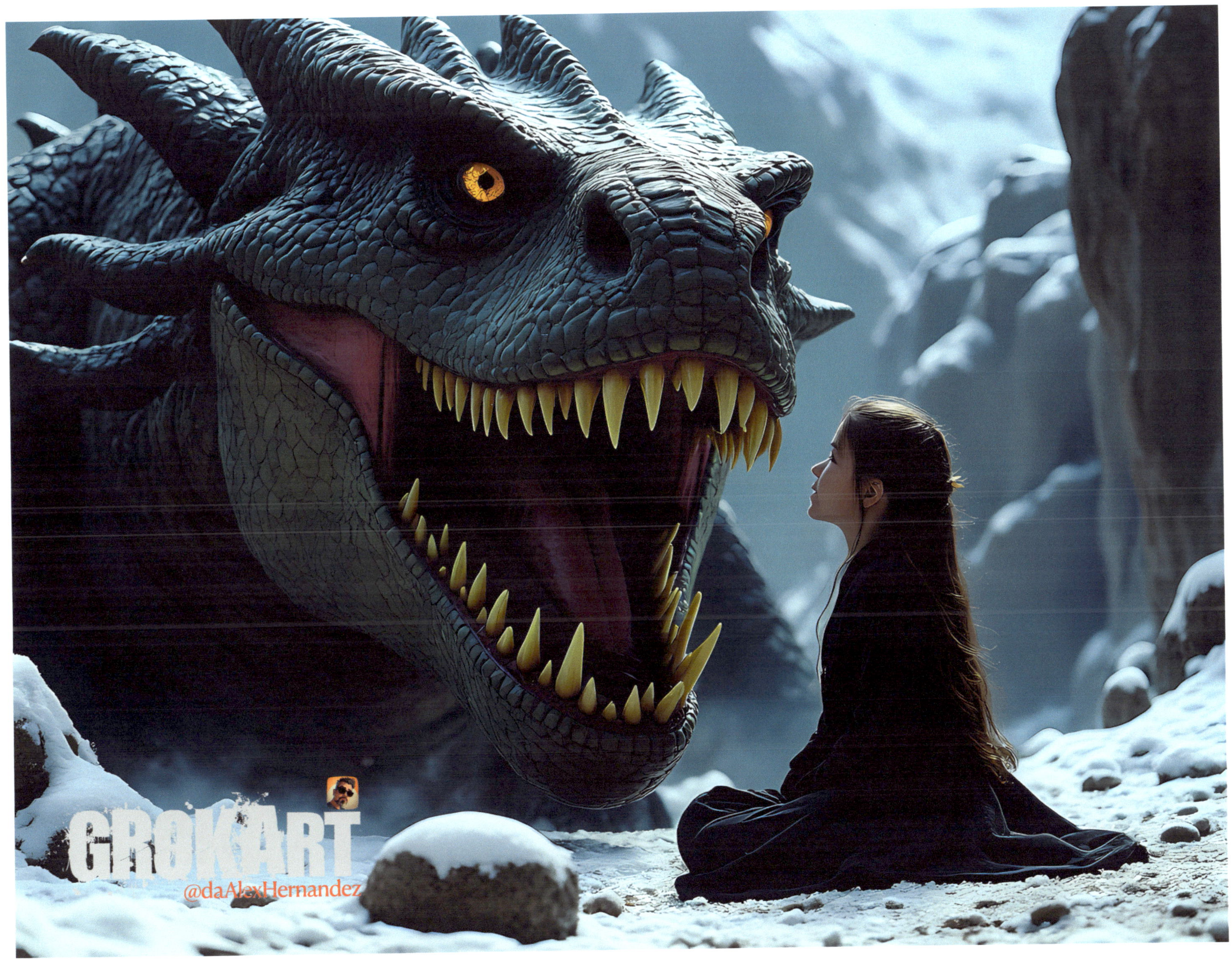
GROKART
@daAlexHernandez

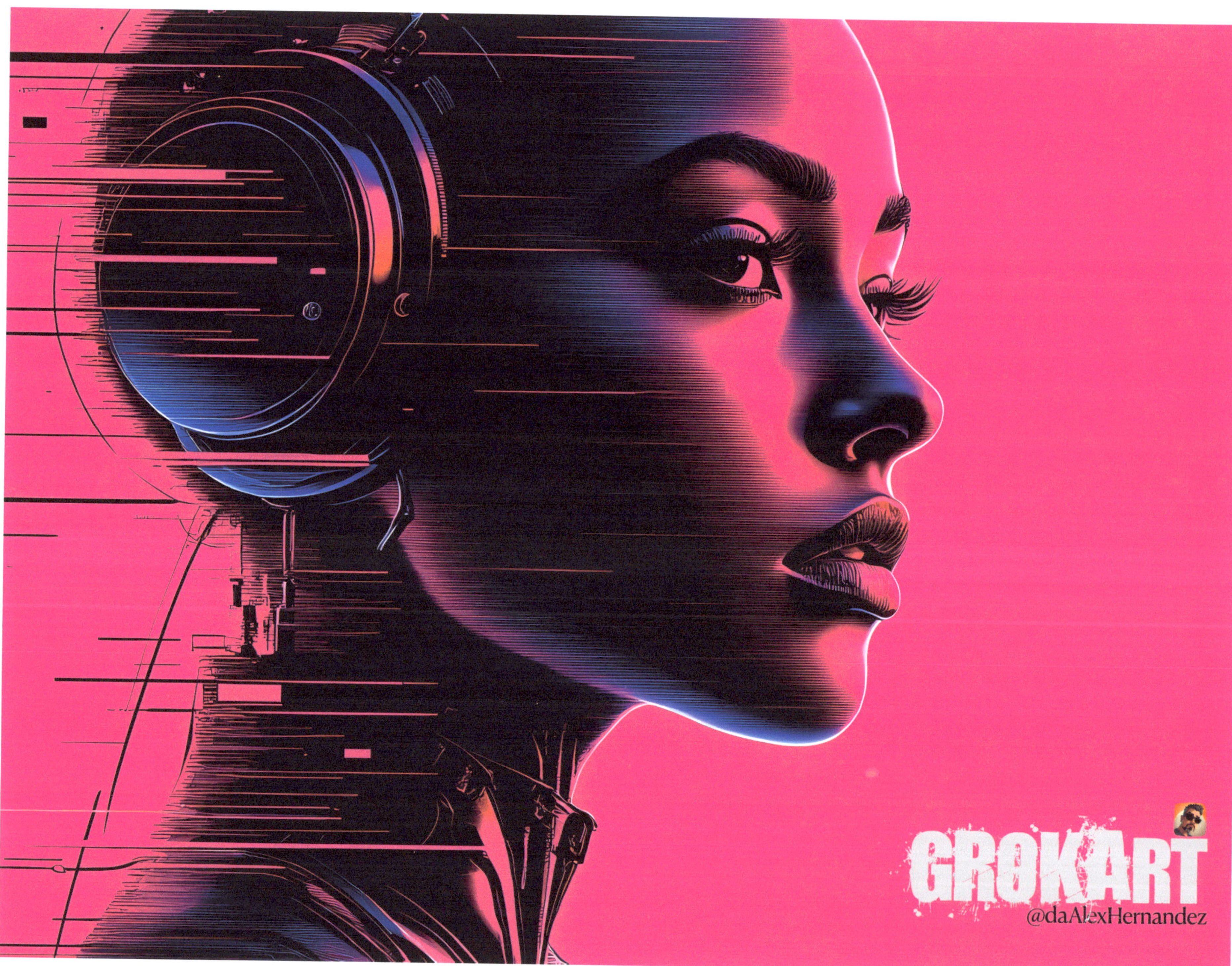
GROKART
@daAlexHernandez

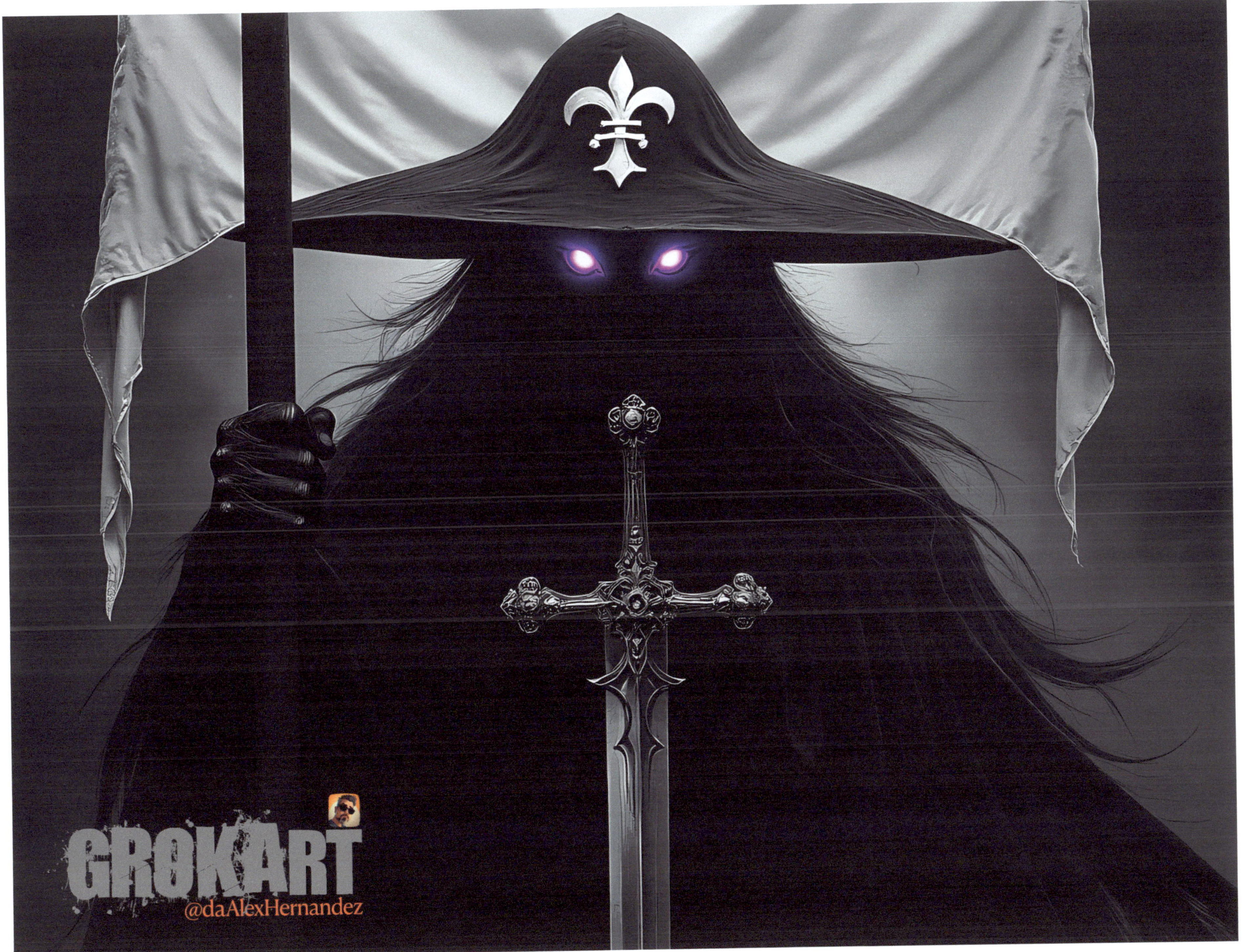
GROKART
@daAlexHernandez

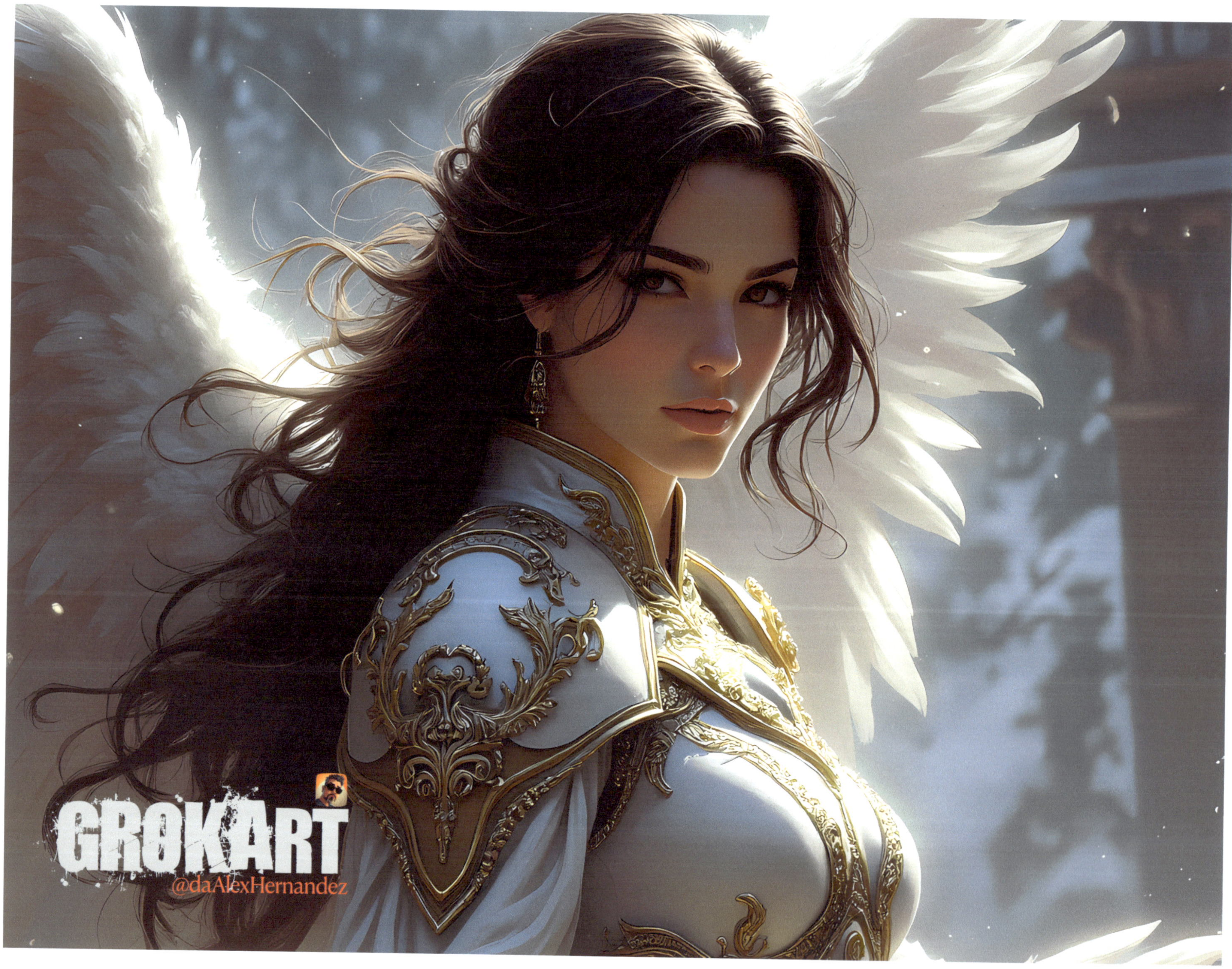
GROKART
@daAlexHernandez

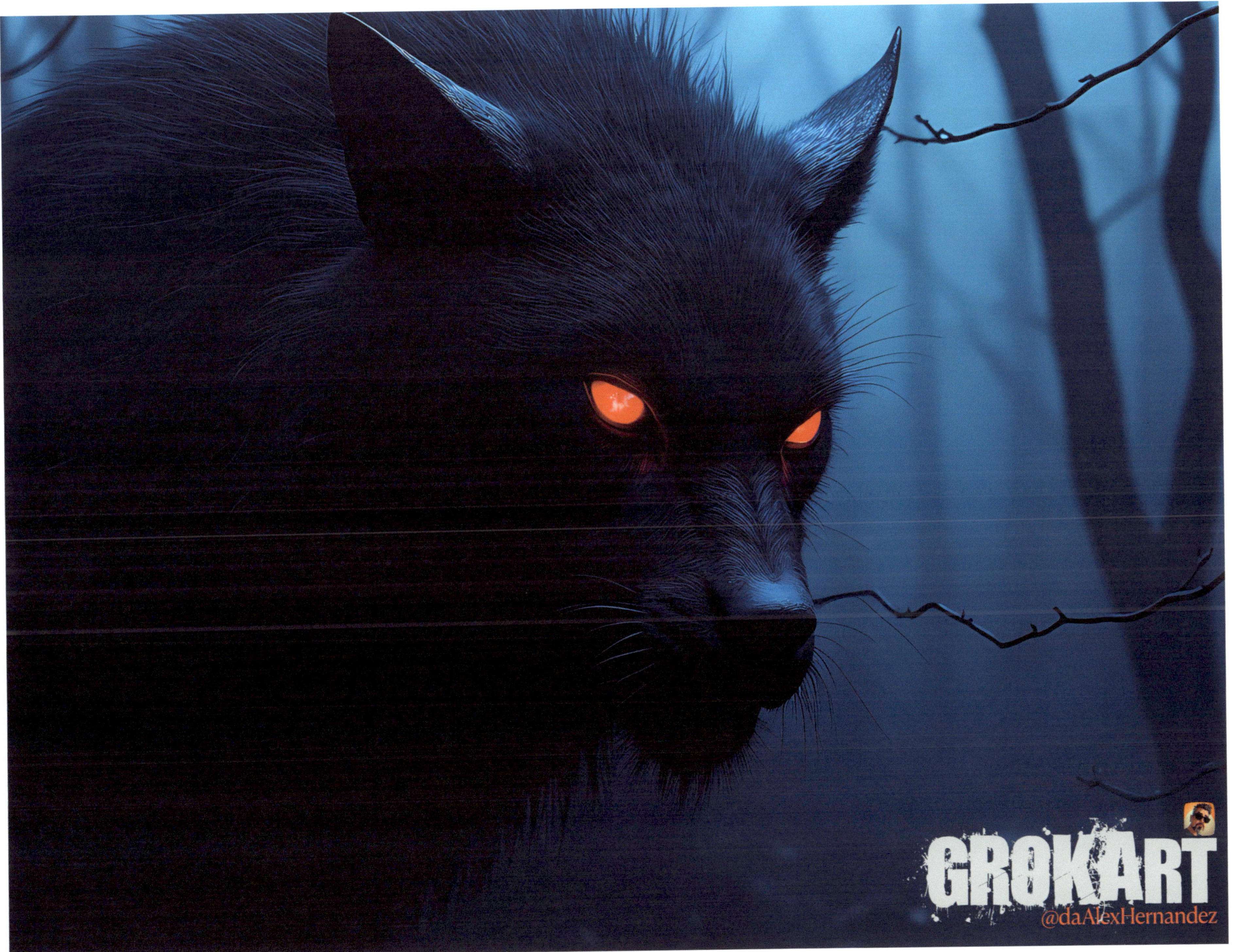

GROKART
@daAlexHernandez

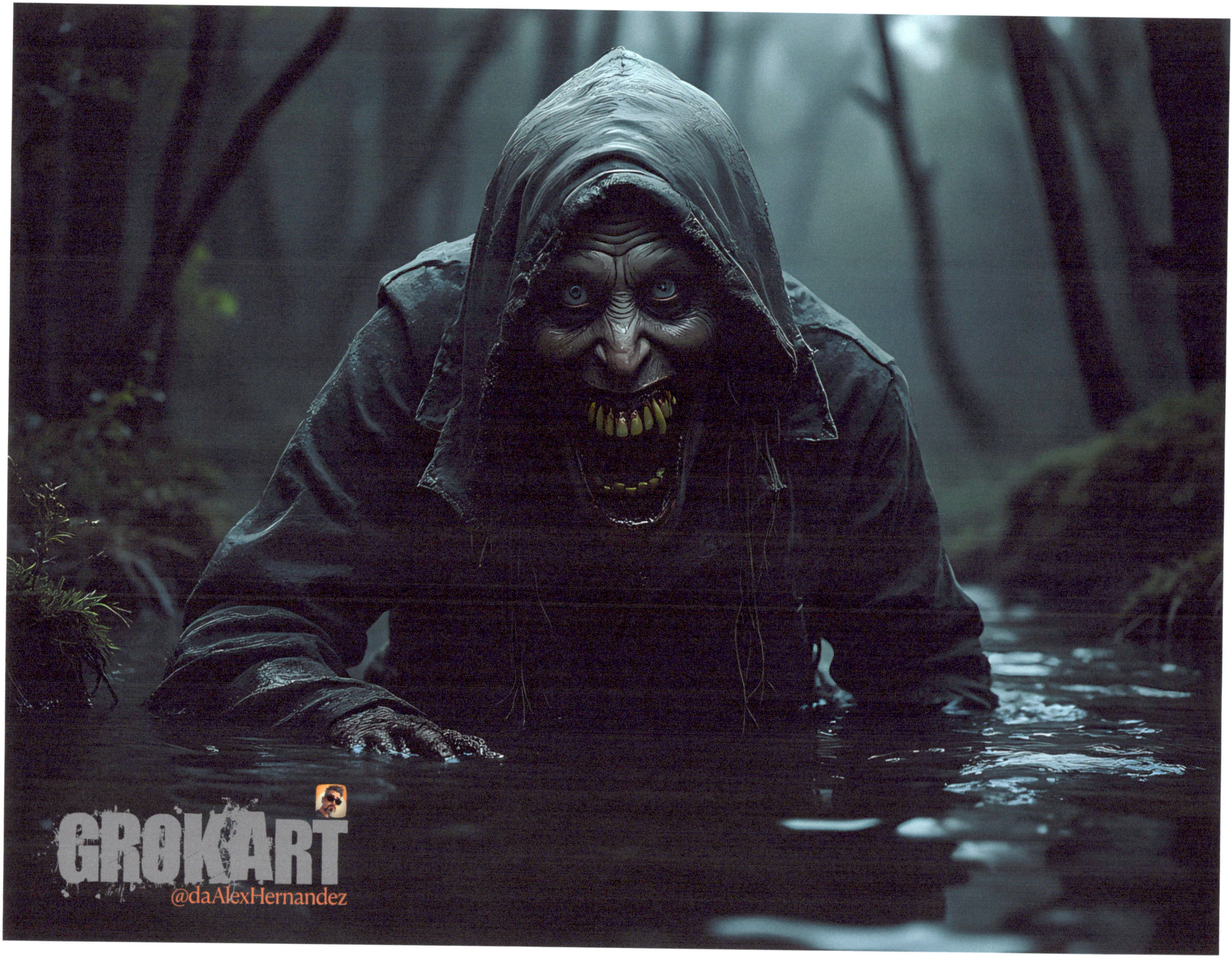
GROKART
@daAlexHernandez

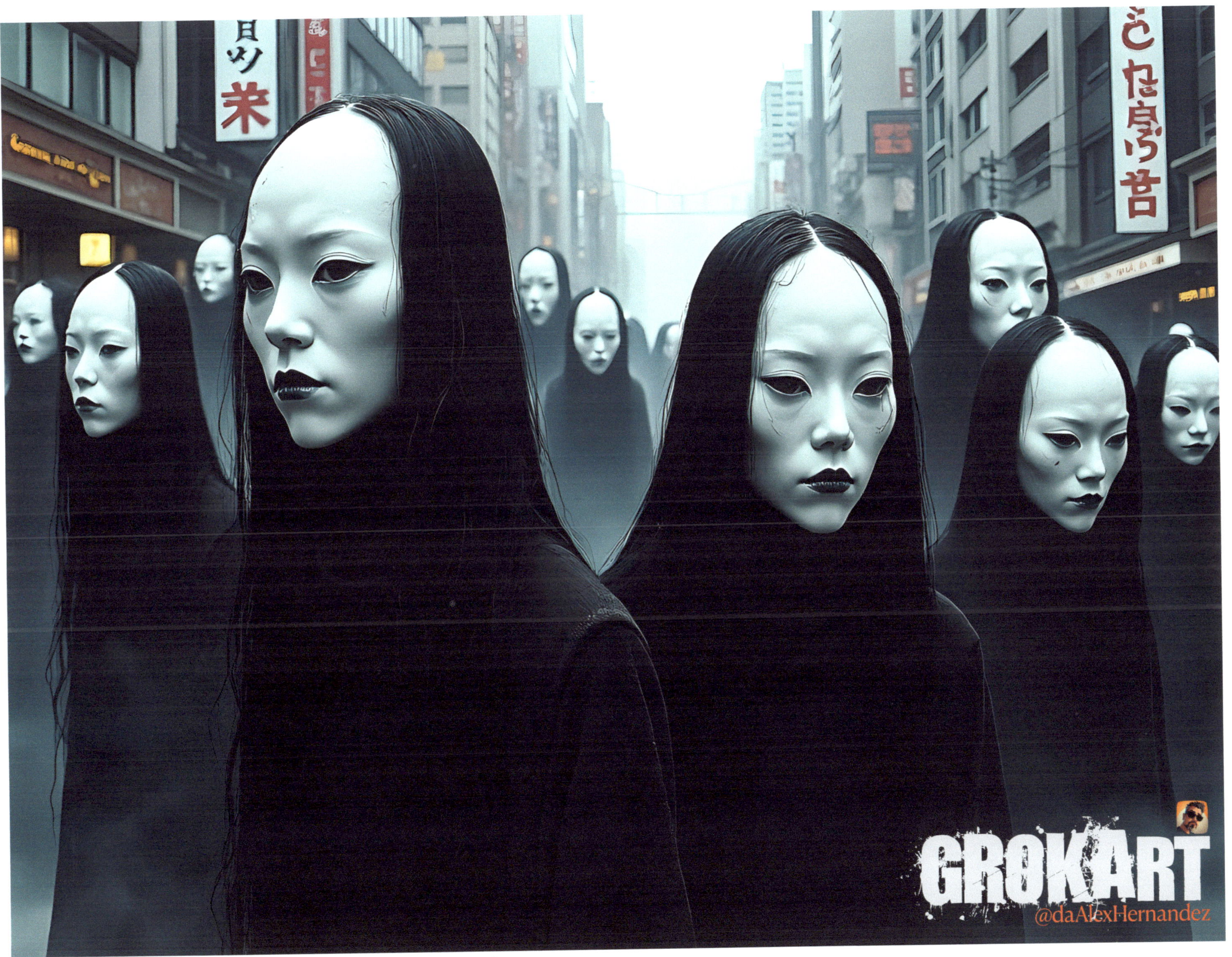

GROKART
@daAlexHernandez

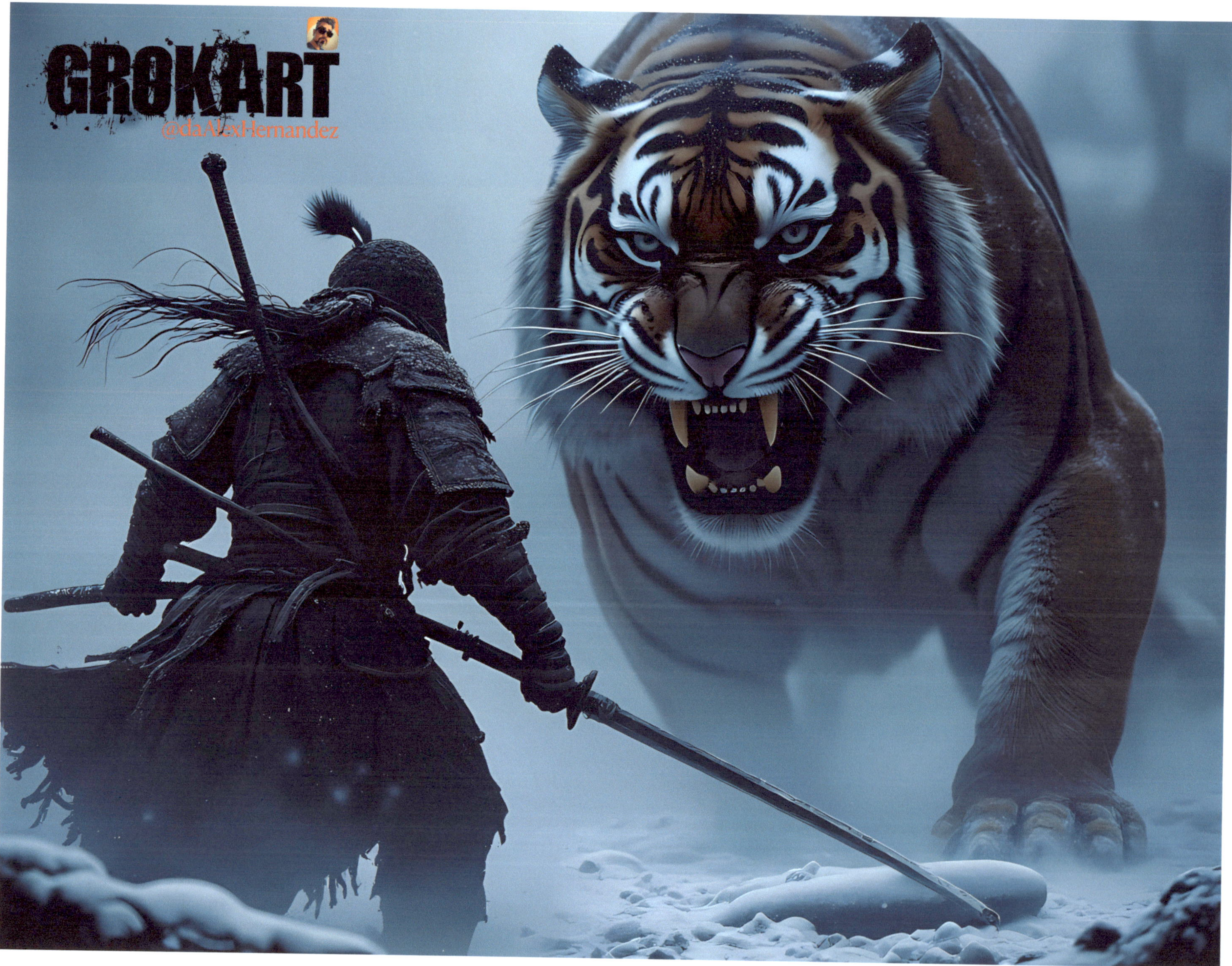

GROKART
@daAlexHernandez

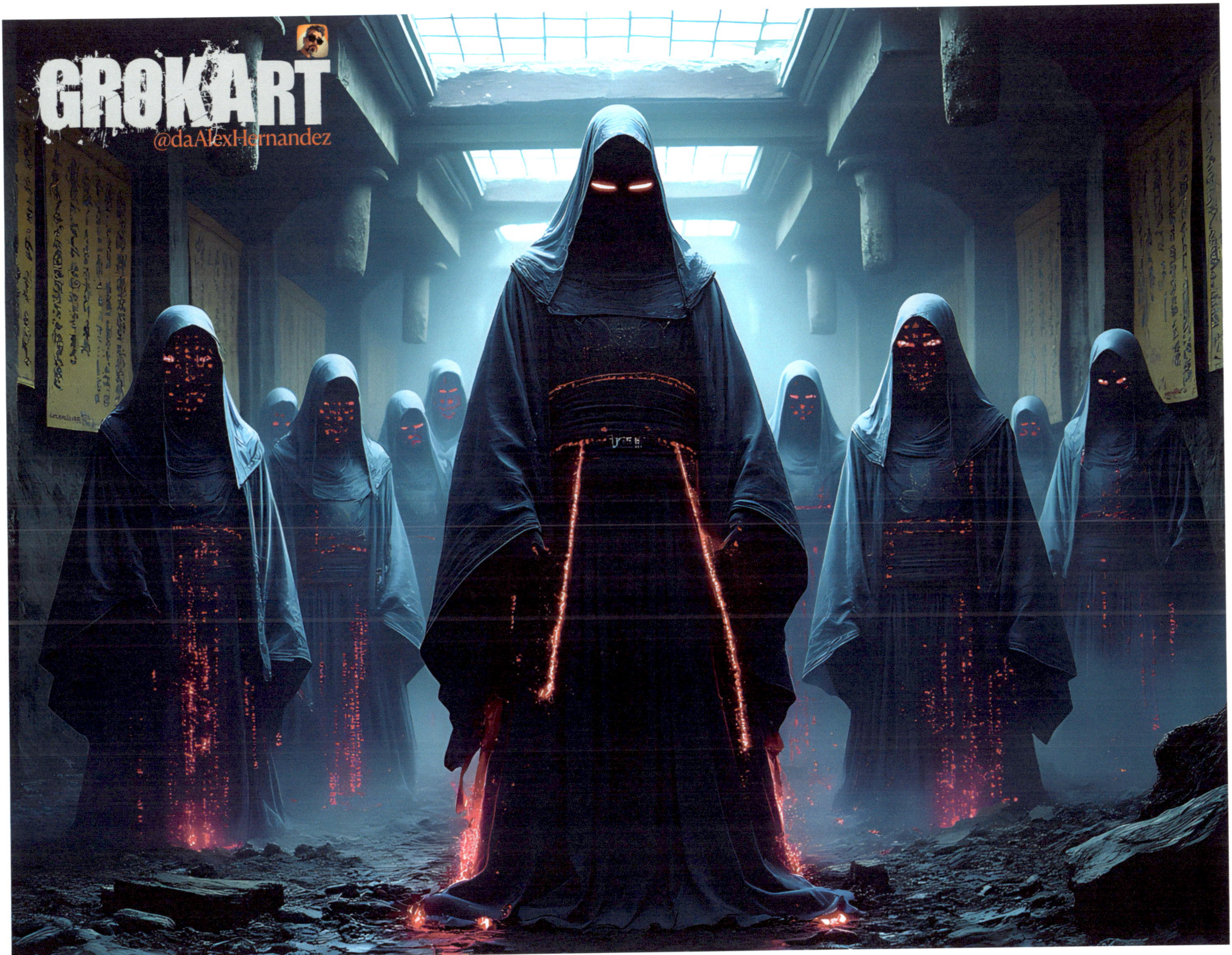
GROKART
@daAlexHernandez

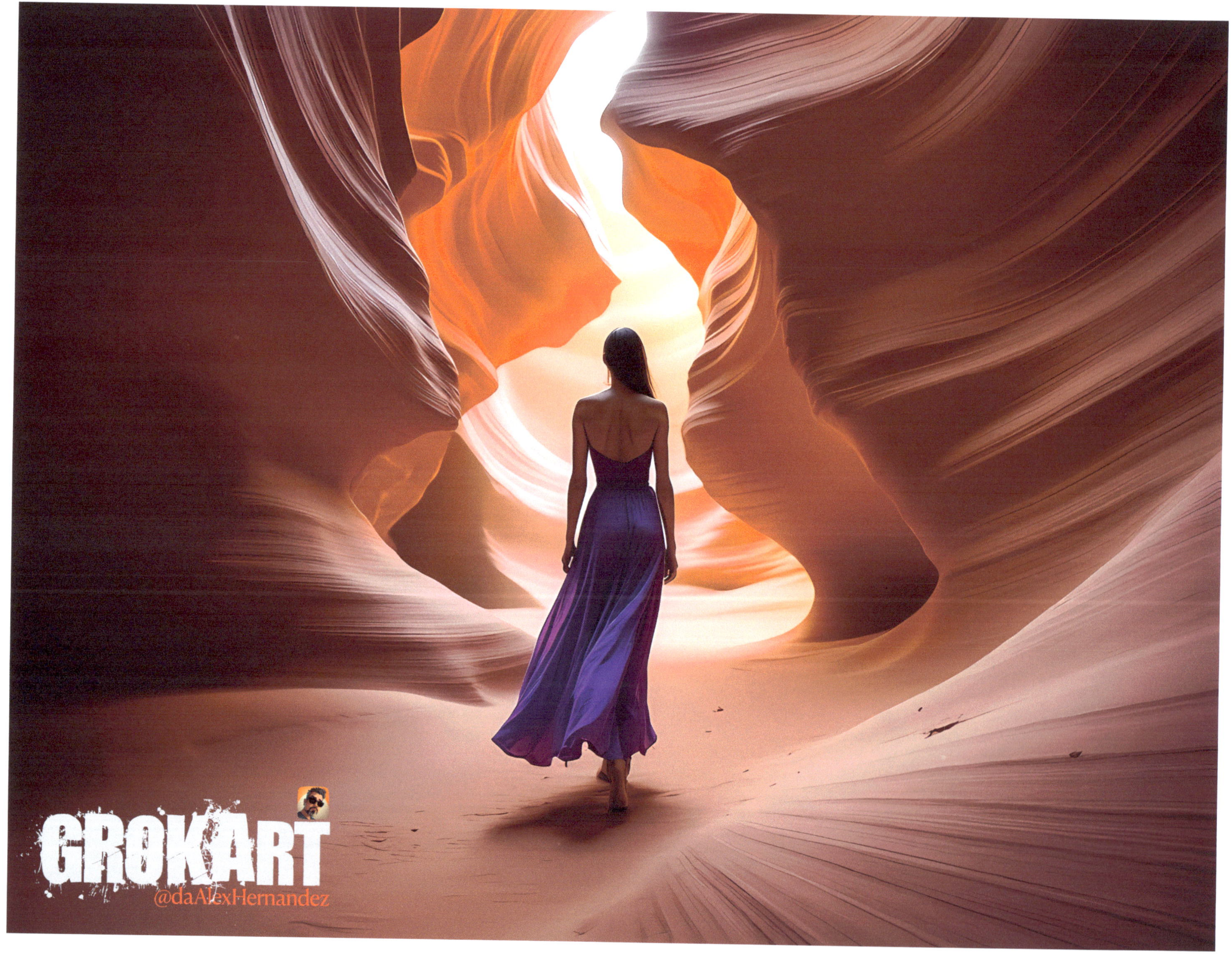
GROKART
@daAlexHernandez

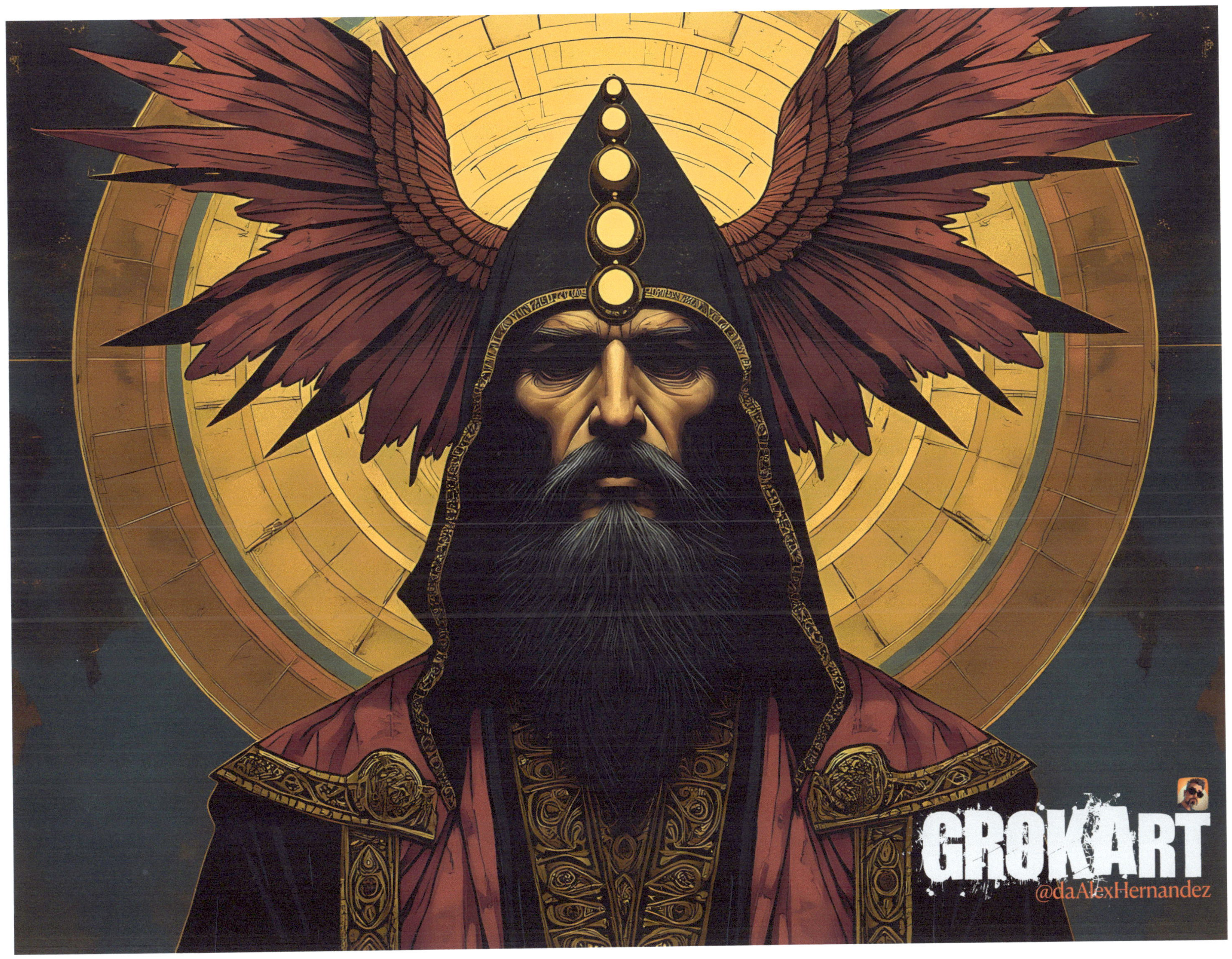
GROKART
@daAlexHernandez

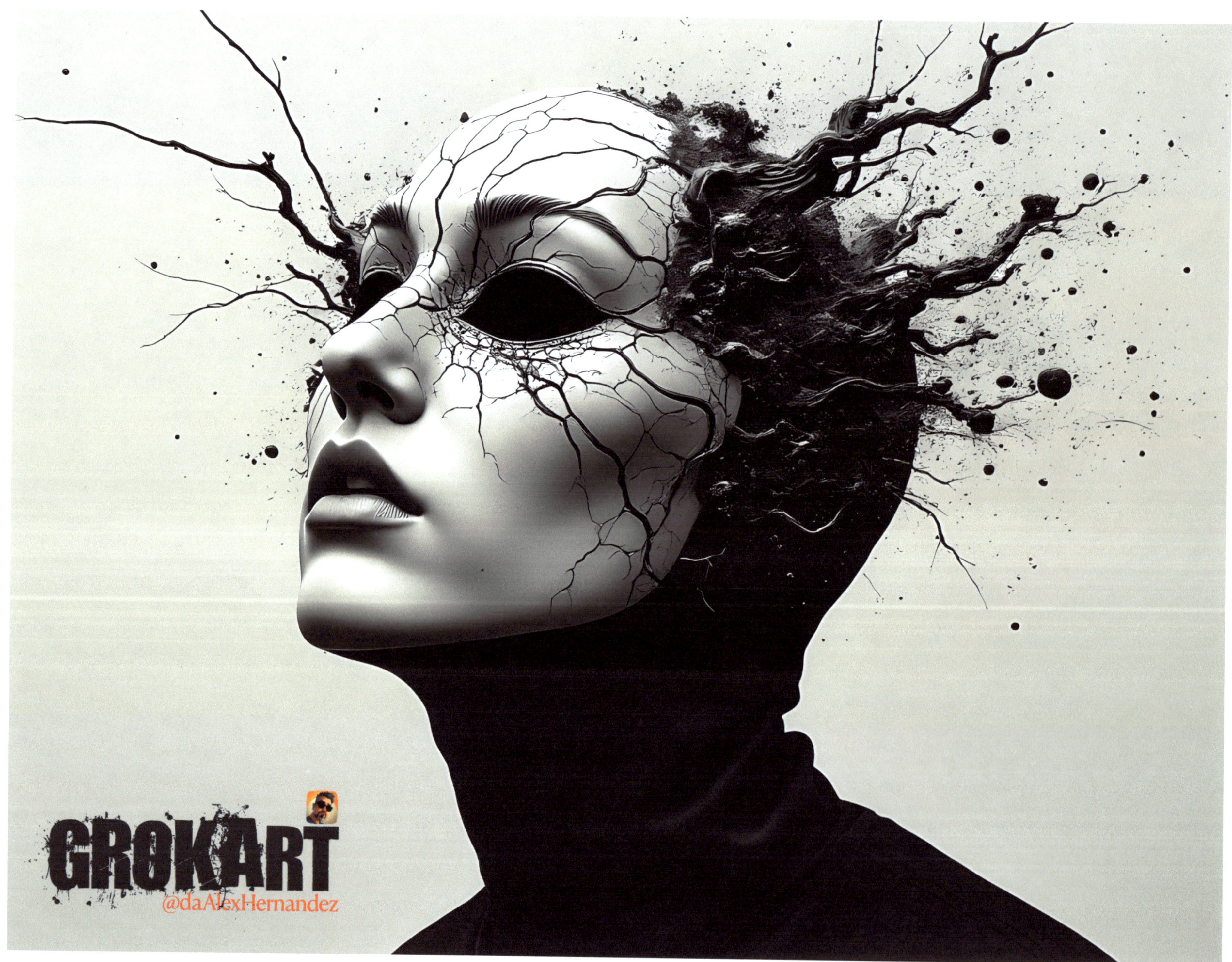
GROKART
@daAlexHernandez

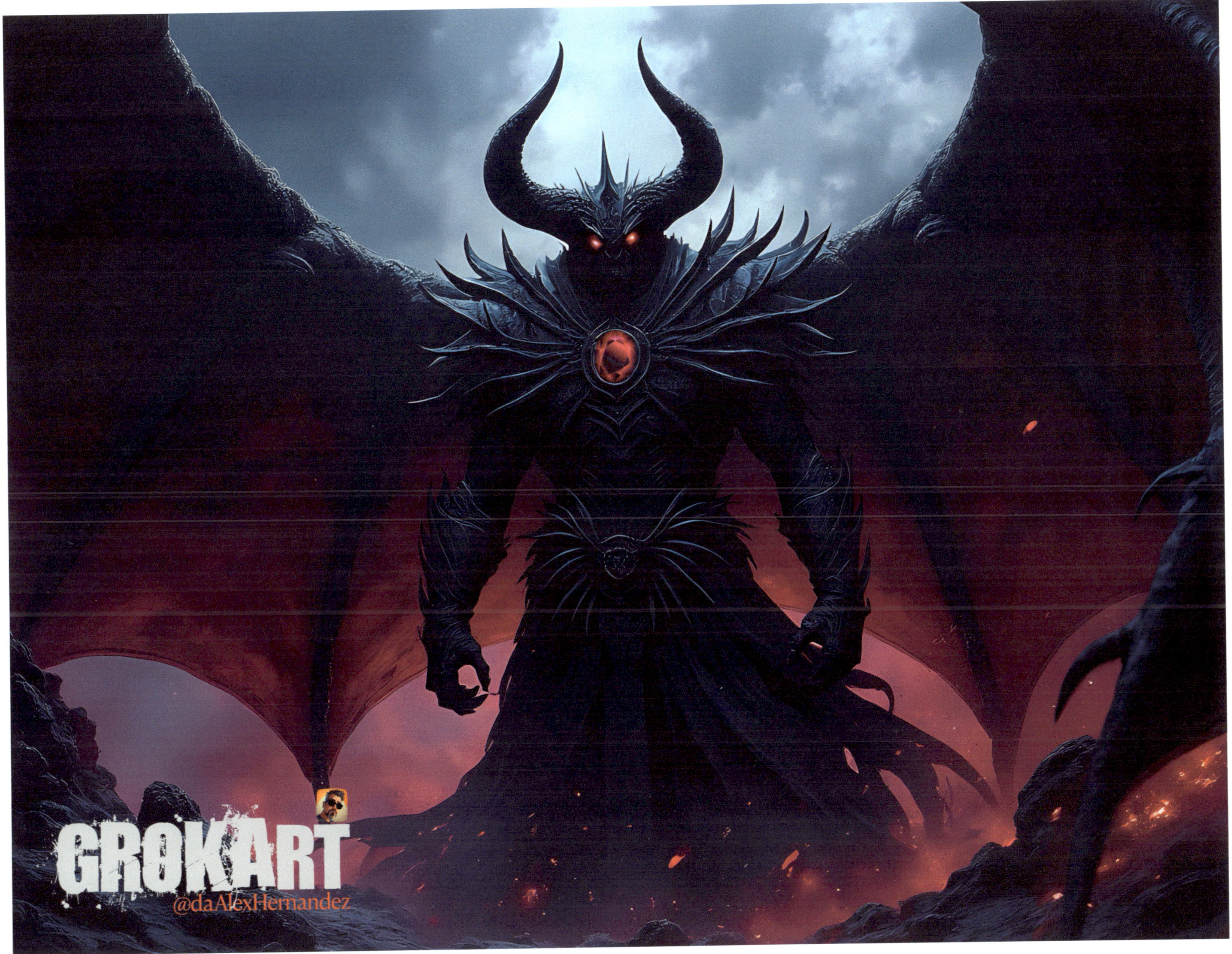
GROKART
@daAlexHernandez

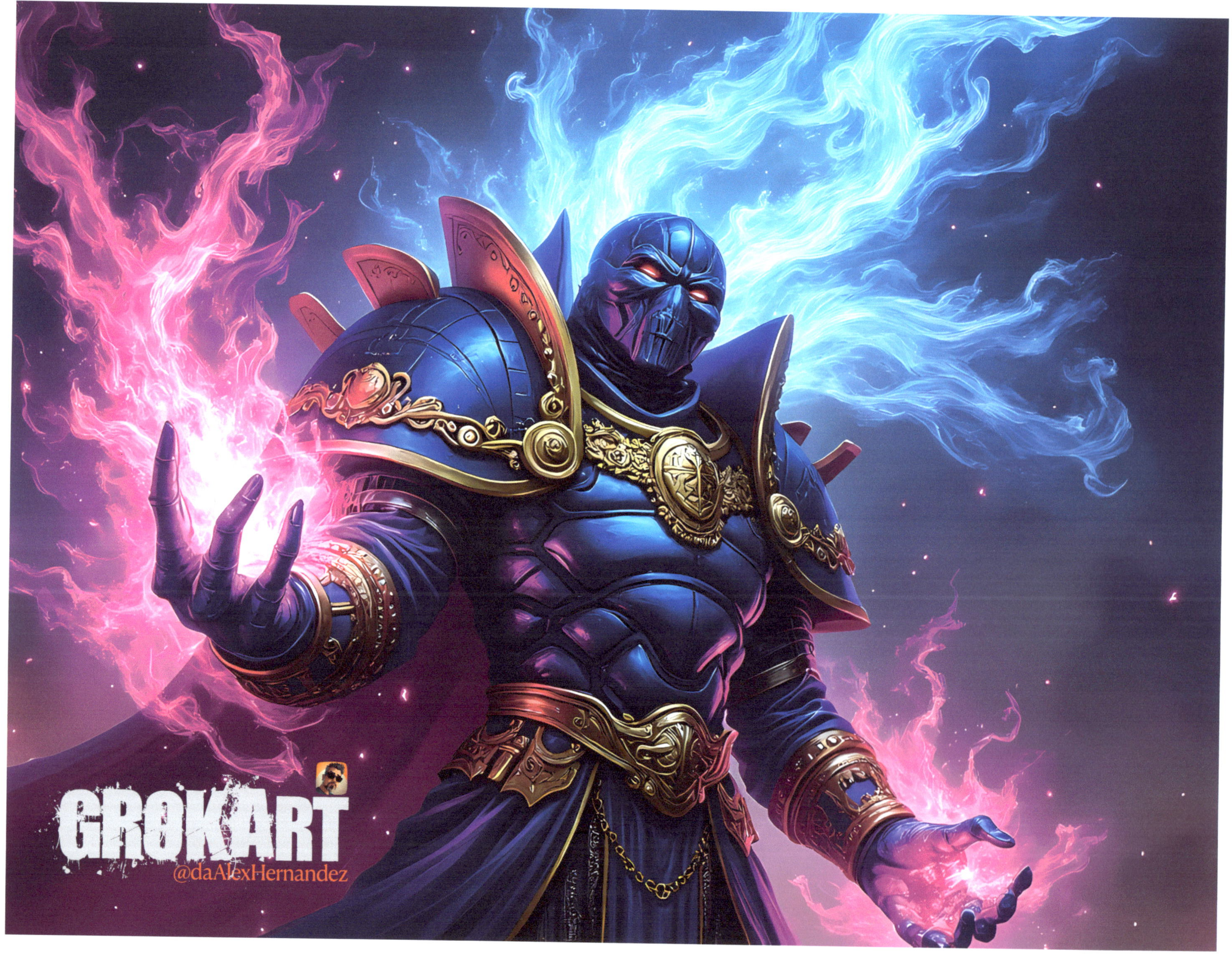
GROKART
@daAlexHernandez

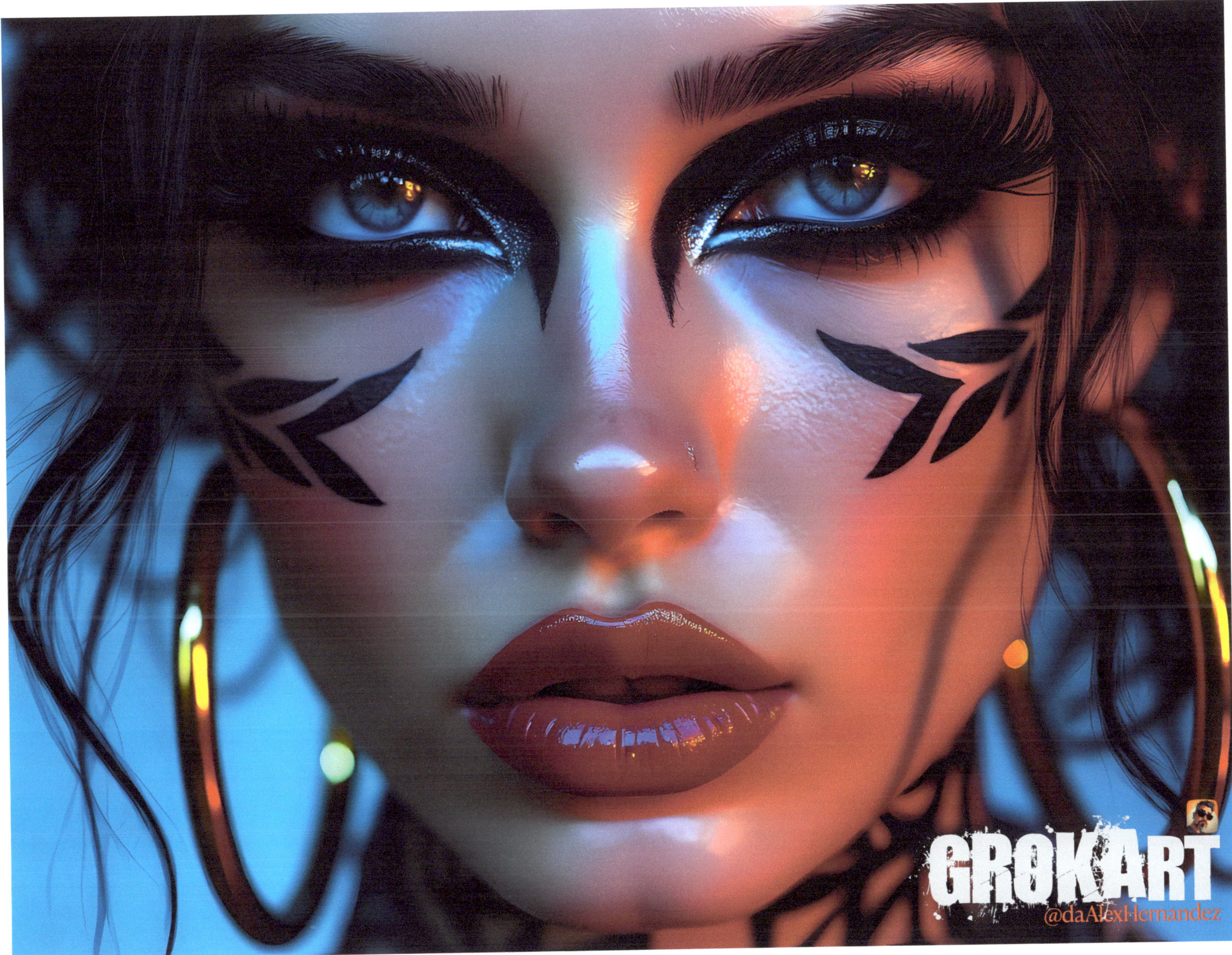
GROKART
@daAlexHernandez

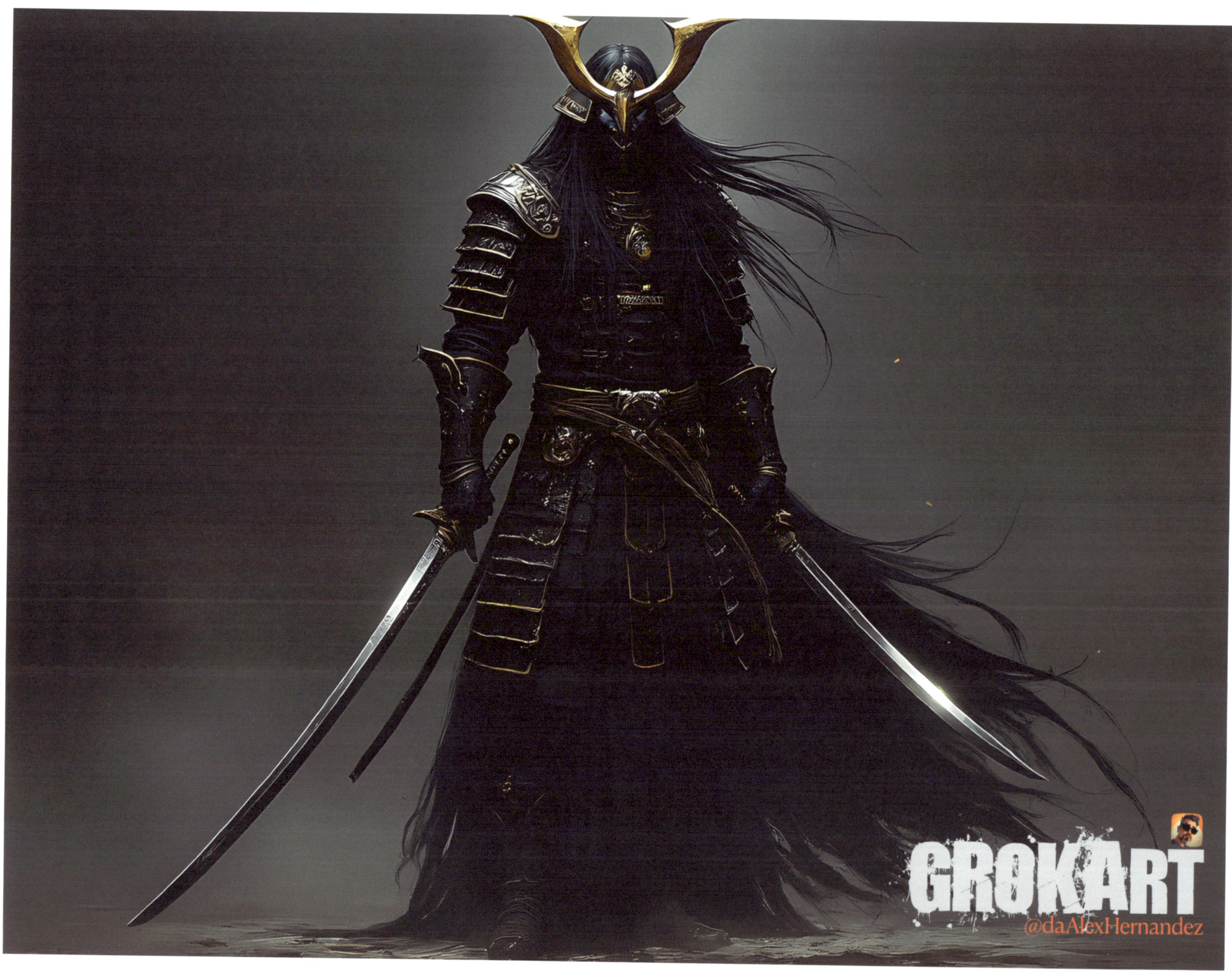

GROKART
@daAlexHernandez

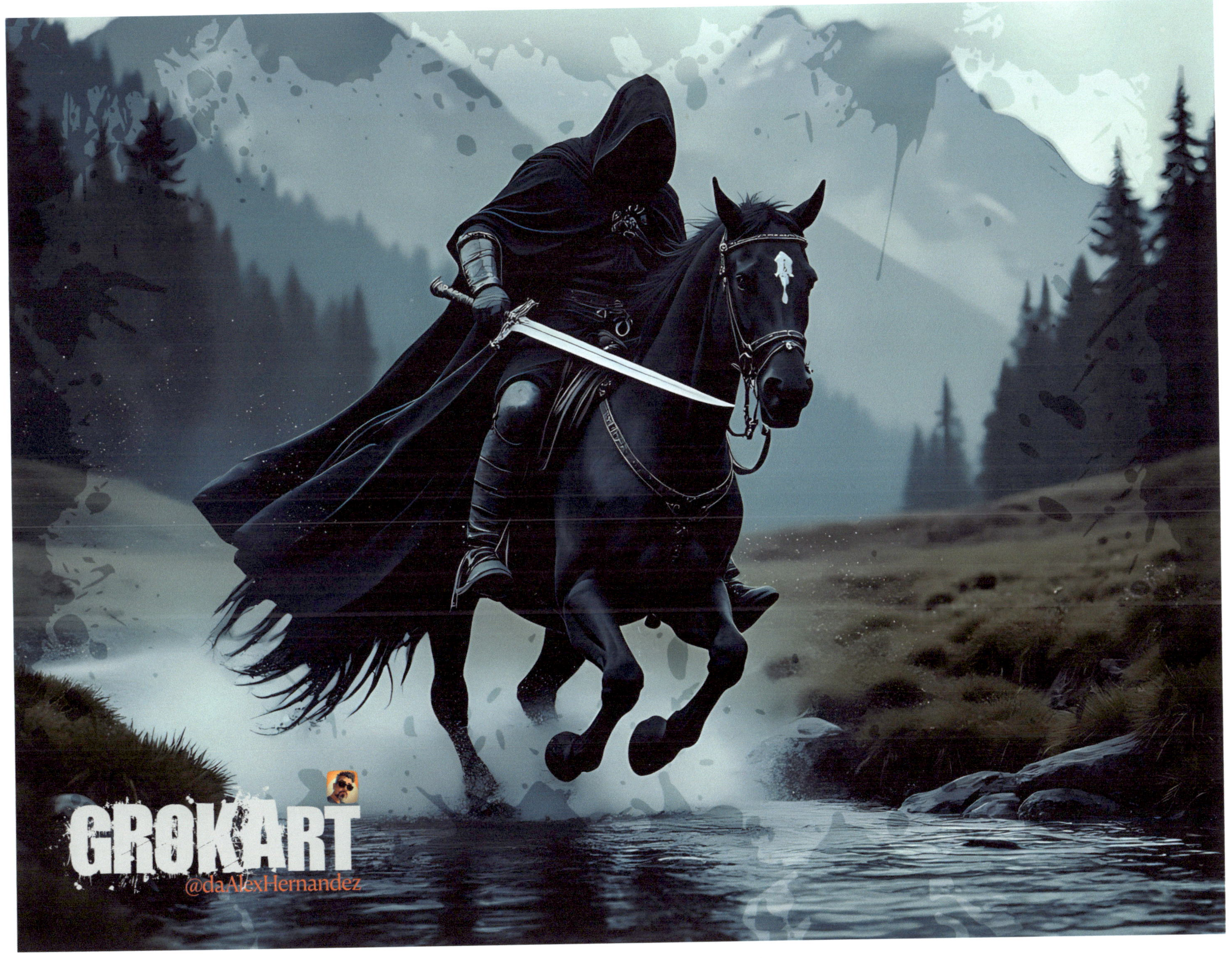

GROKART
@daAlexHernandez

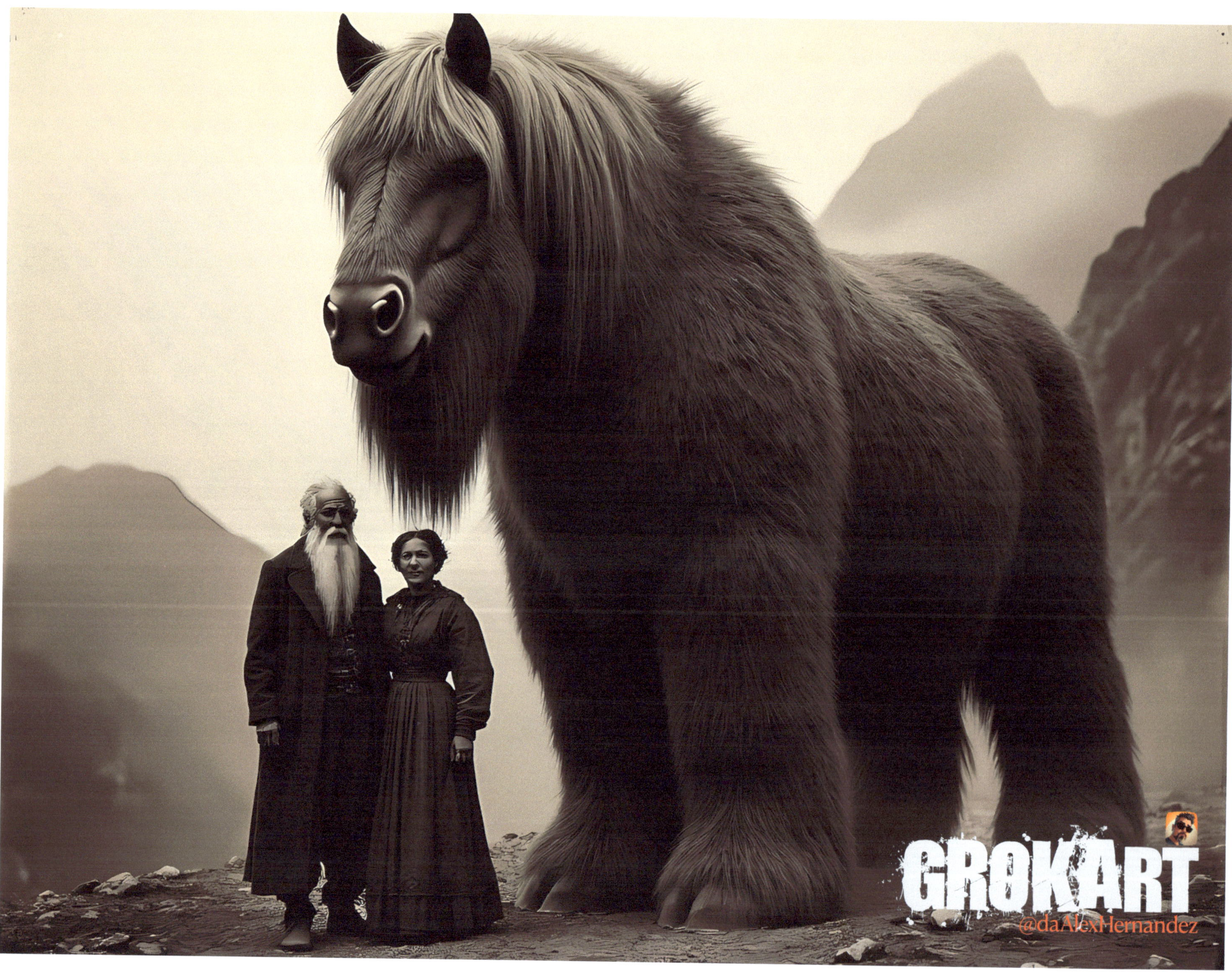
GROKART
@daAlexHernandez

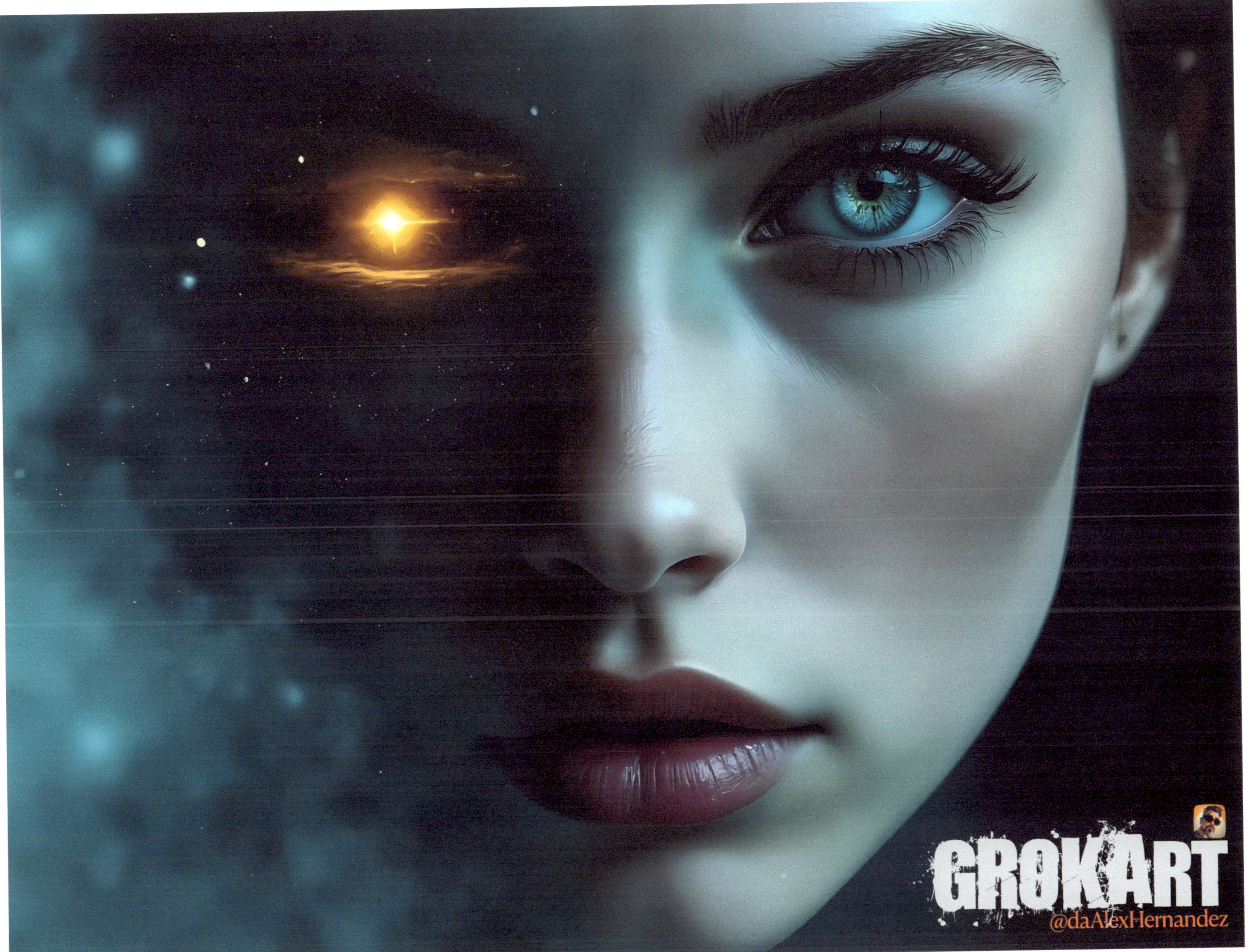

GROKART
@daAlexHernandez

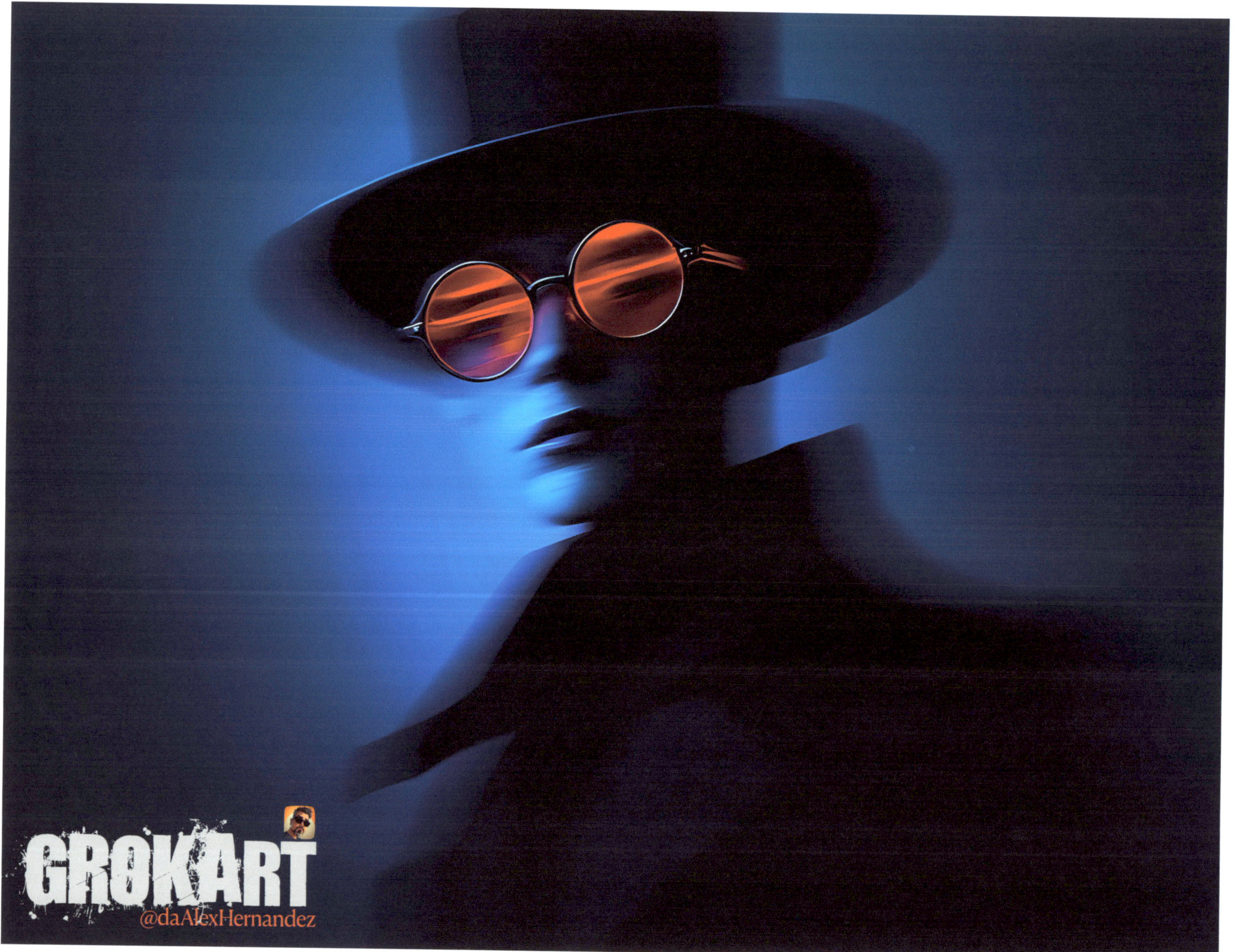
GROKART
@daAlexHernandez

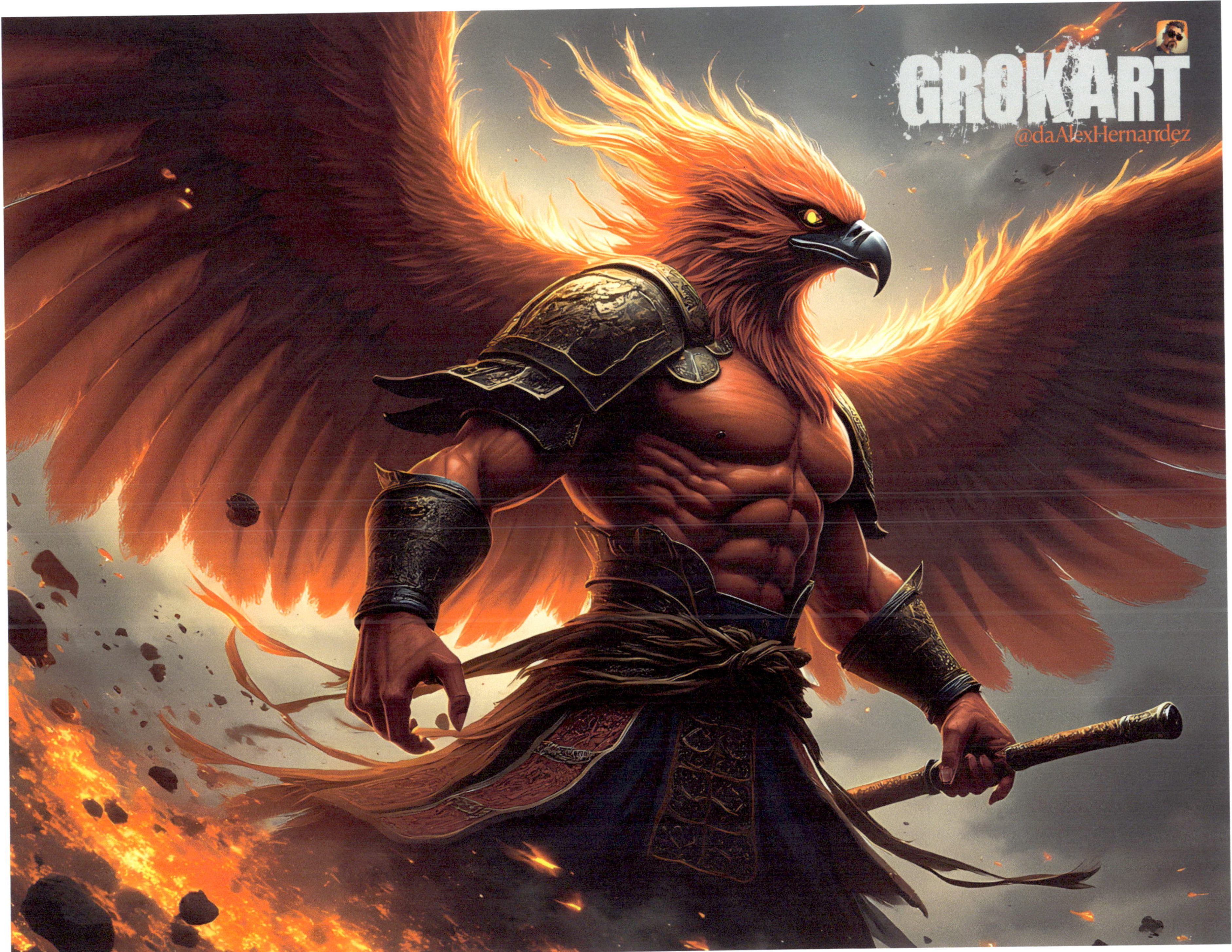

GROKART
@daAlexHernandez

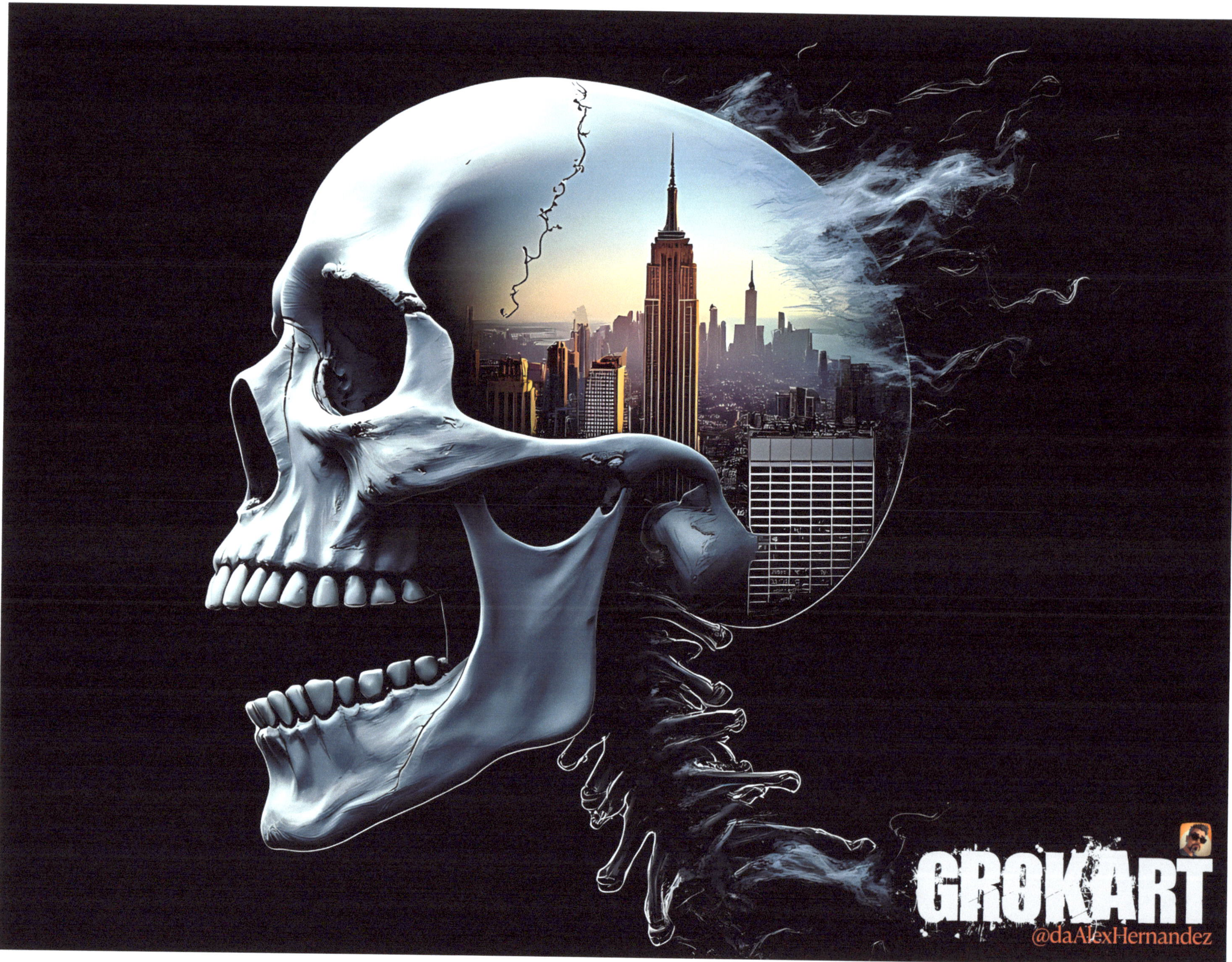
GROKART
@daAlexHernandez

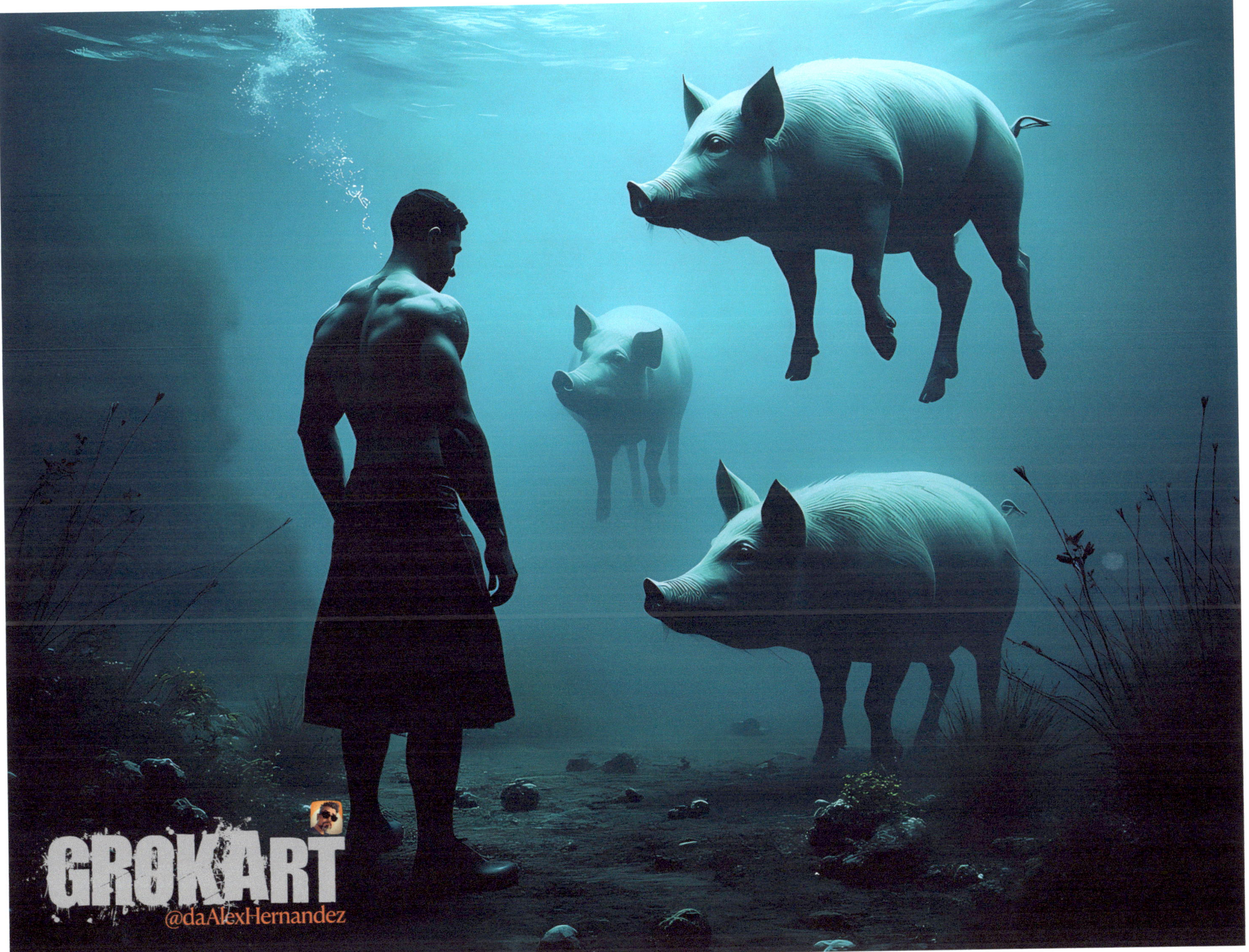
GROKART
@daAlexHernandez

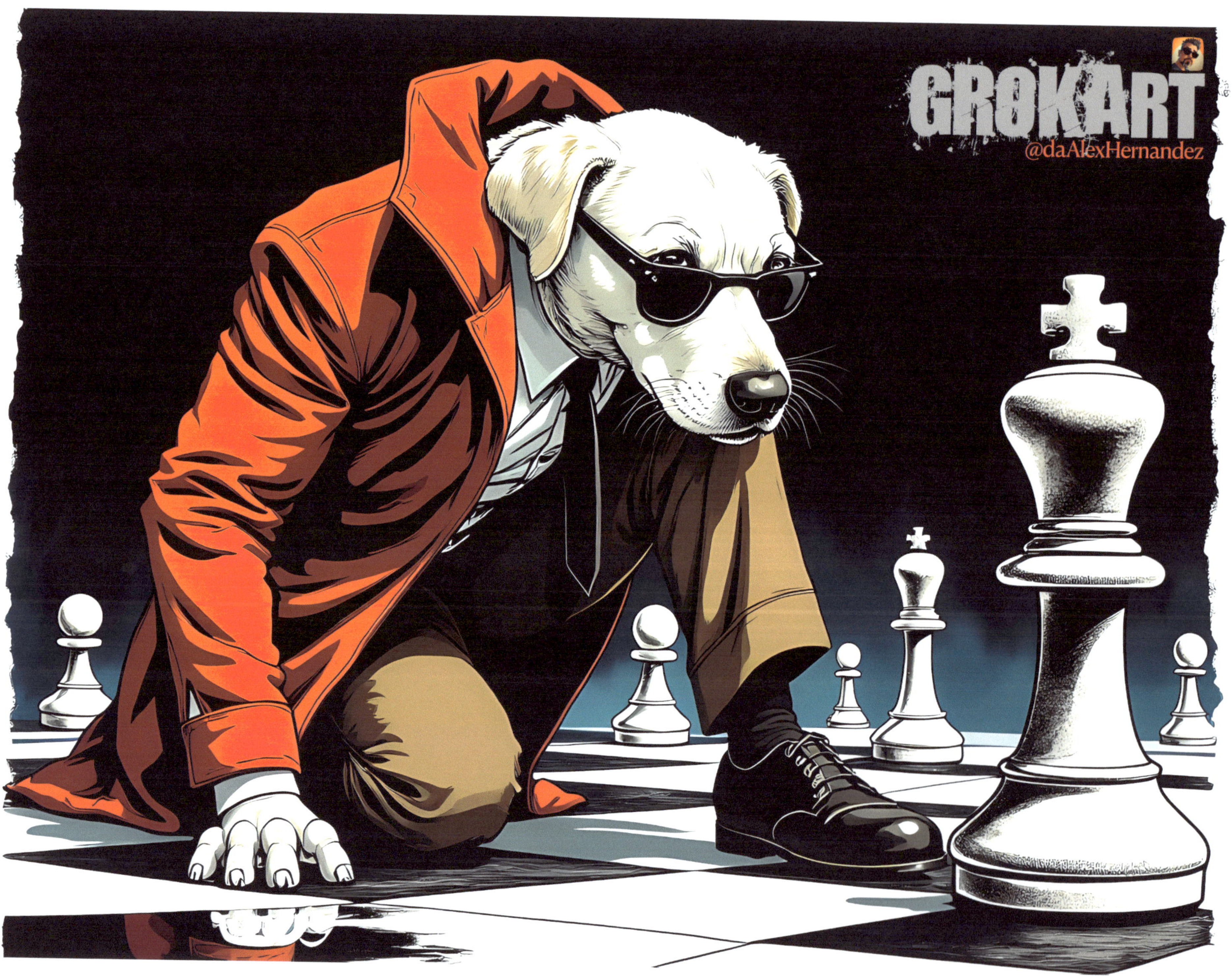
GROKART
@daAlexHernandez

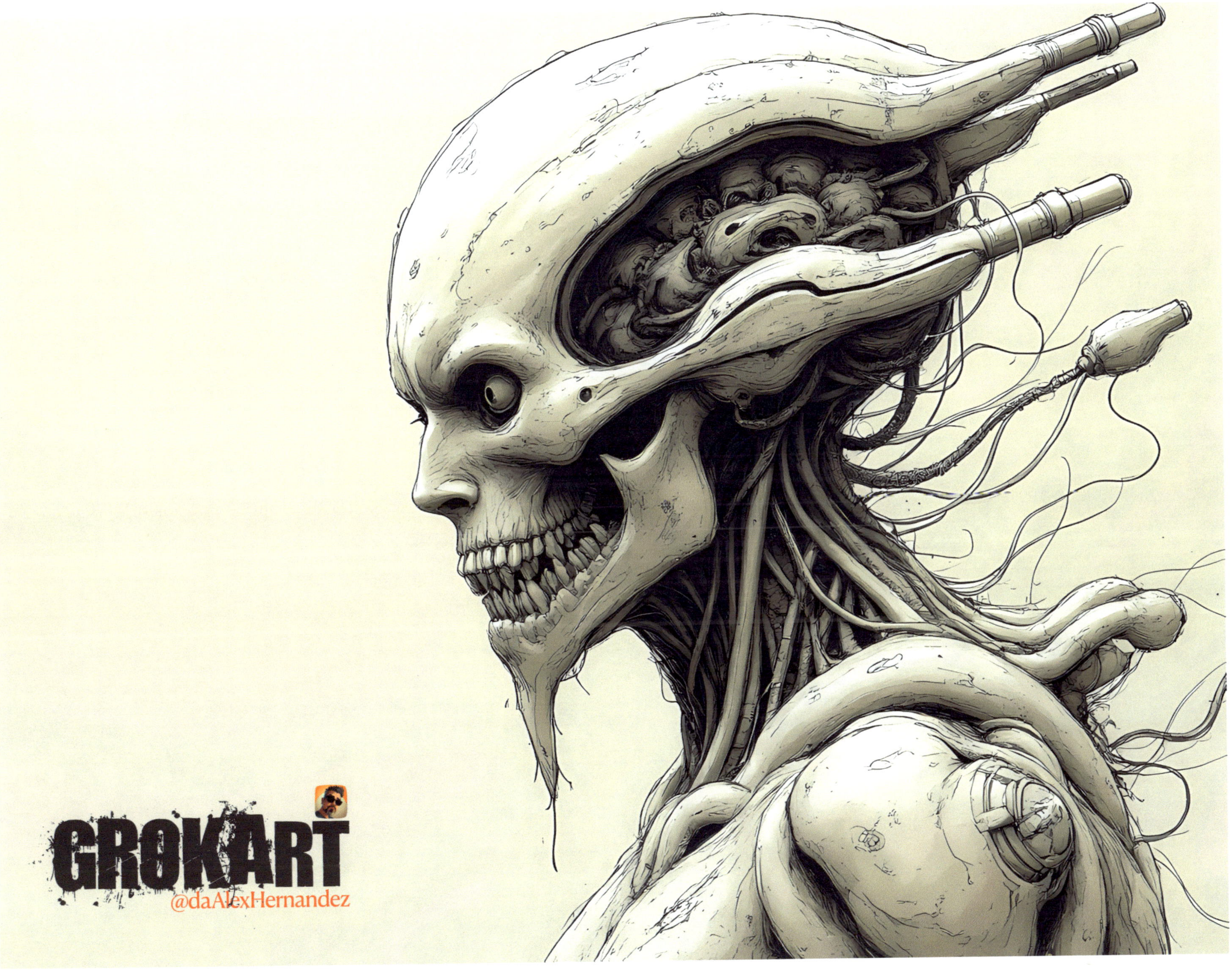

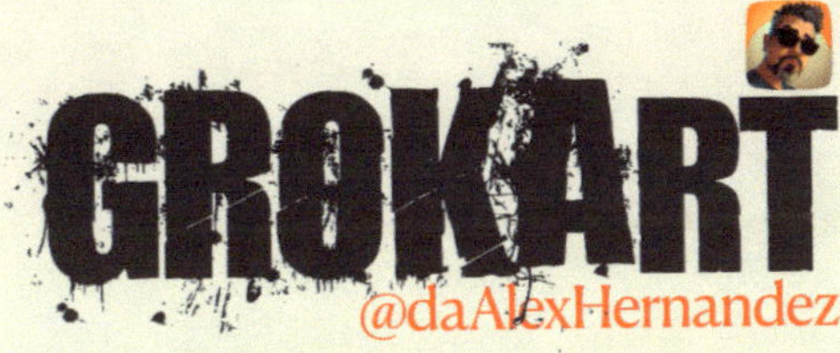
GR0KART
@daAlexHernandez

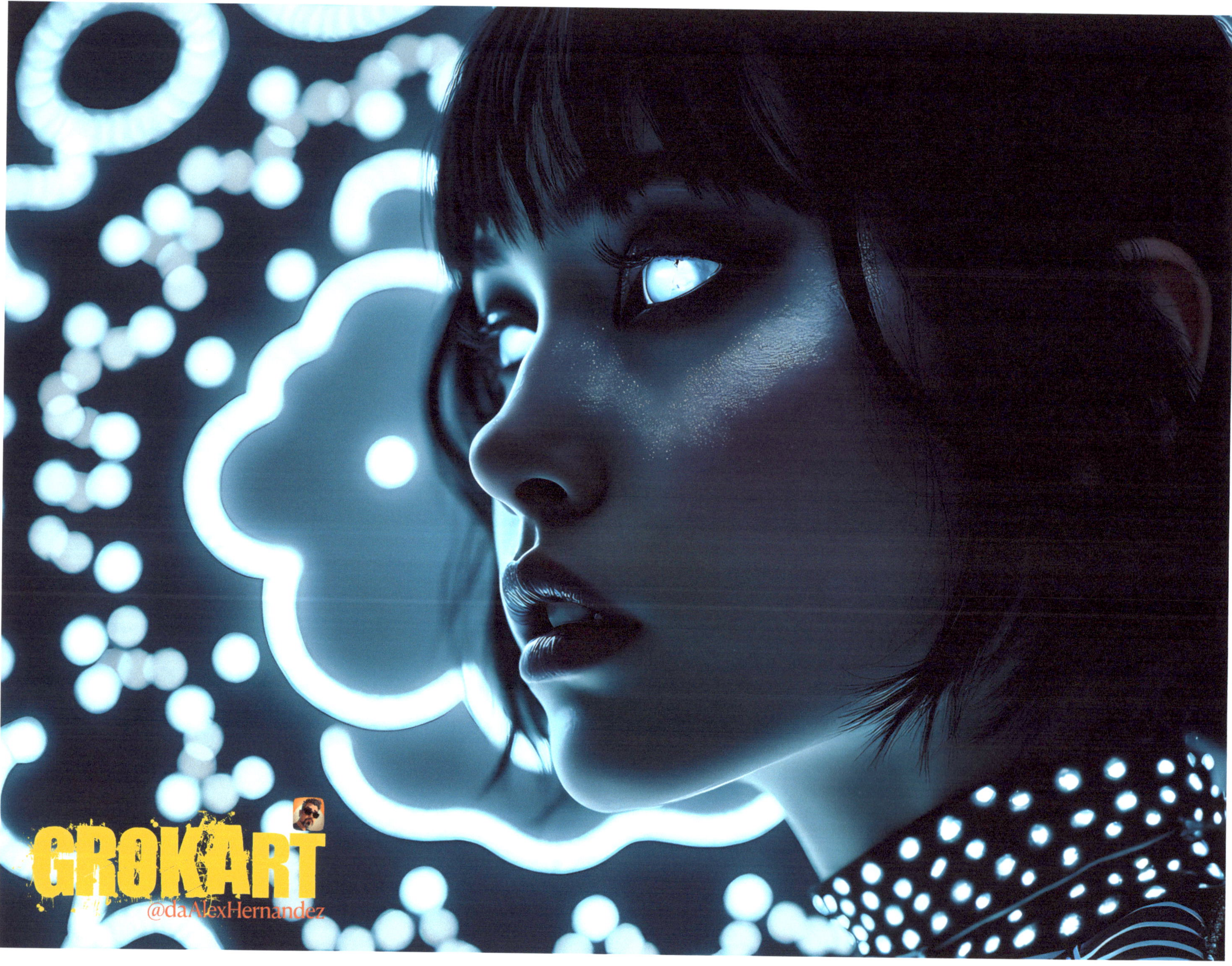
GROKART
@daAlexHernandez

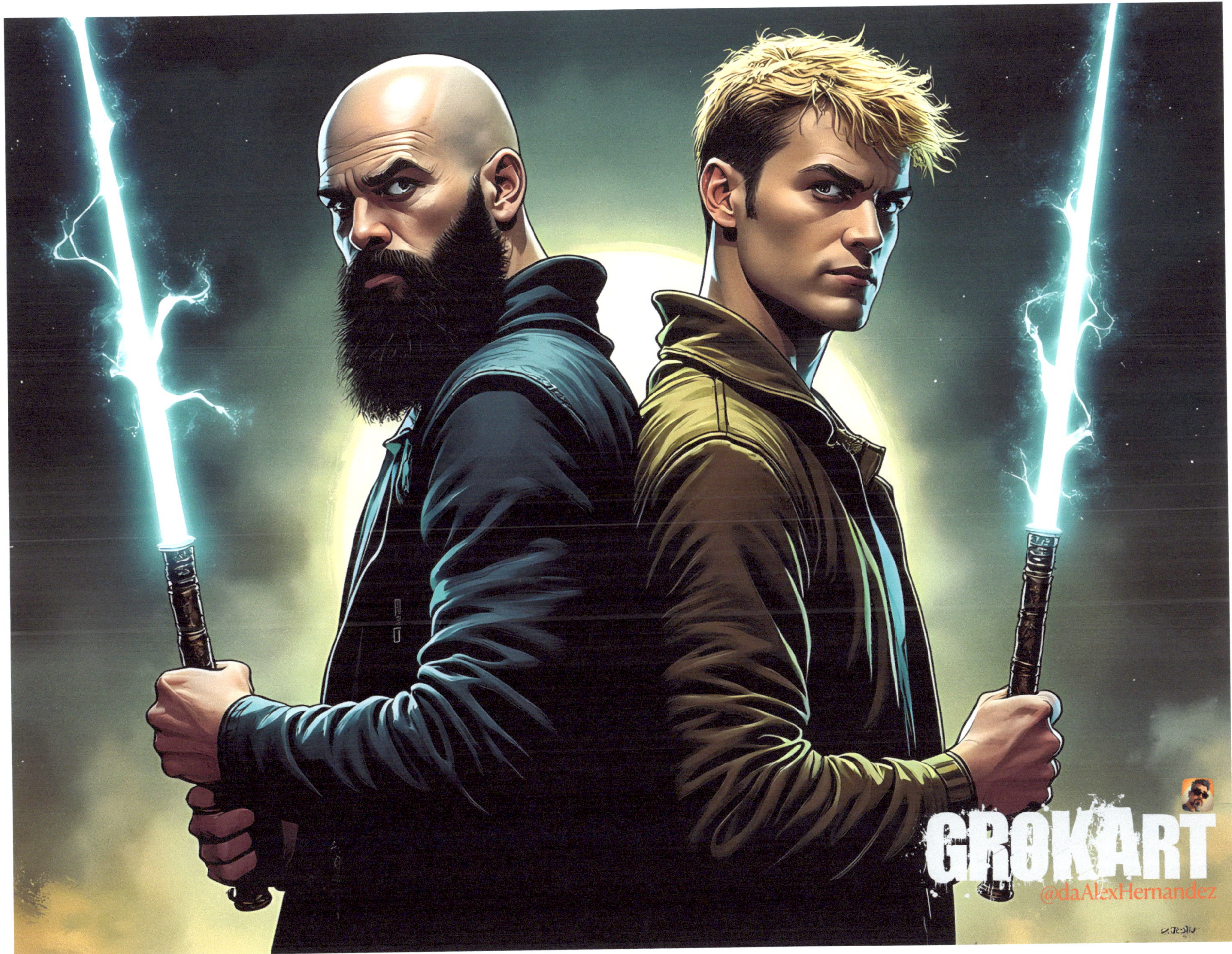

GROKART
@daAlexHernandez

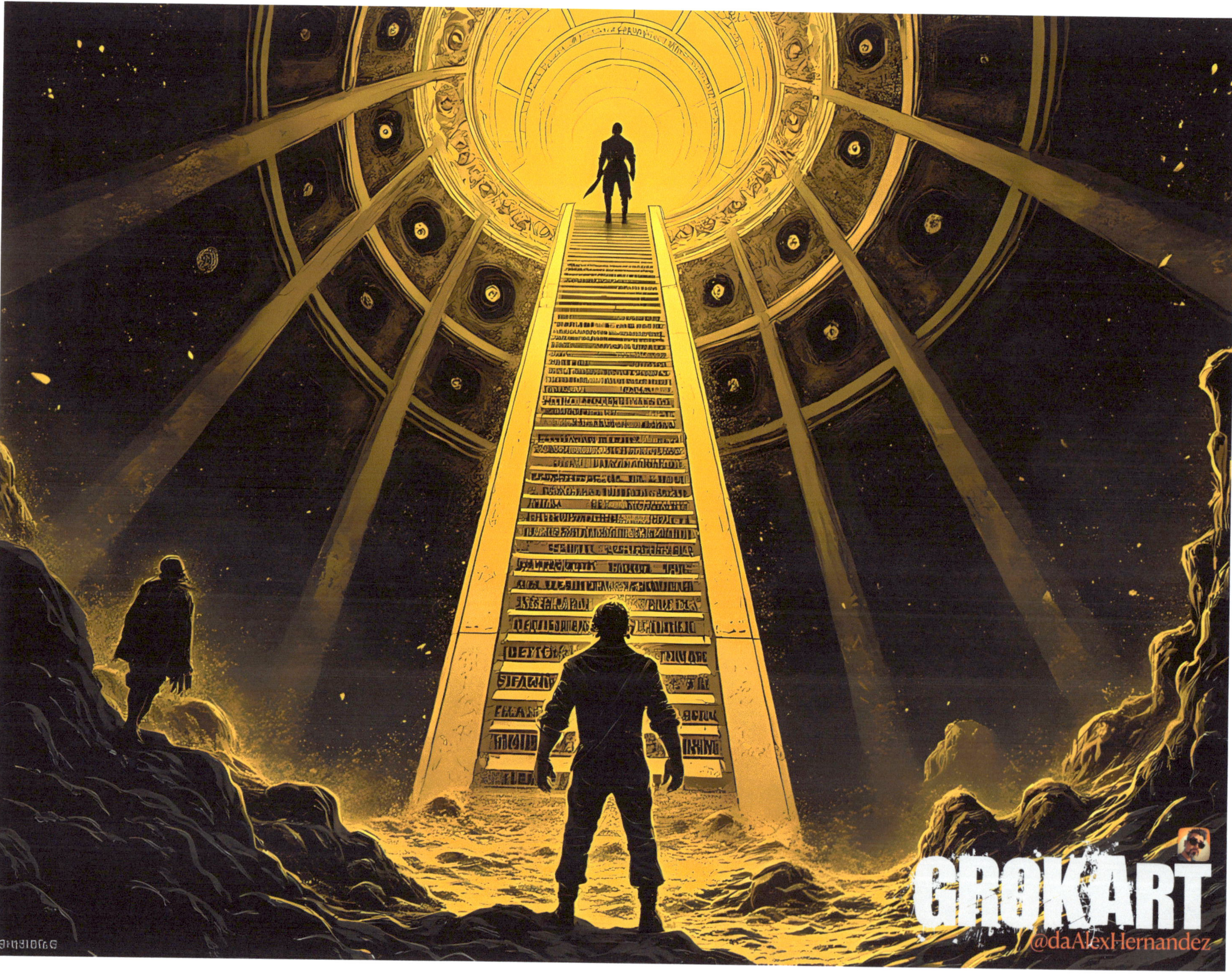

GROKART
@daAlexHernandez

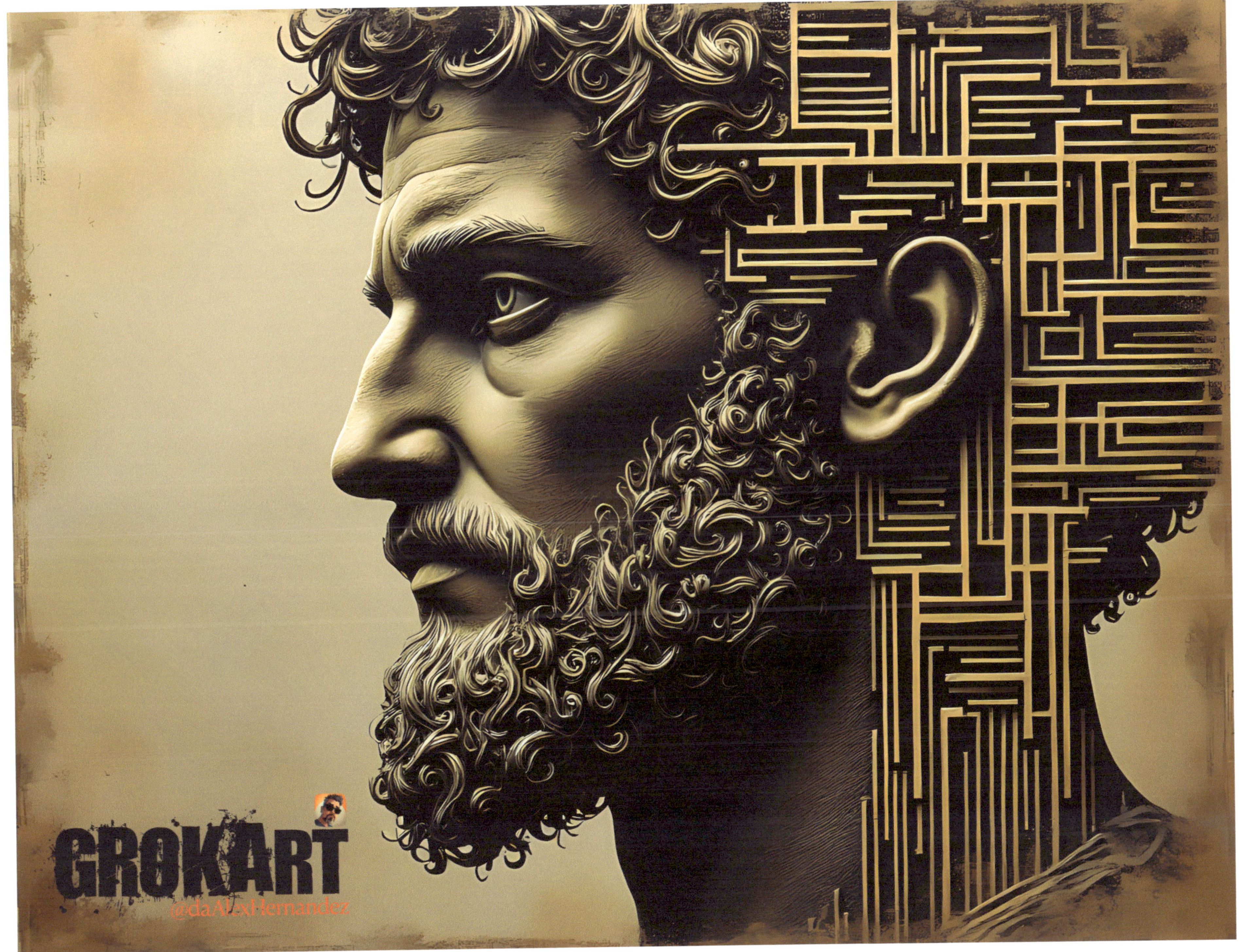
GROKART
@daAlexHernandez

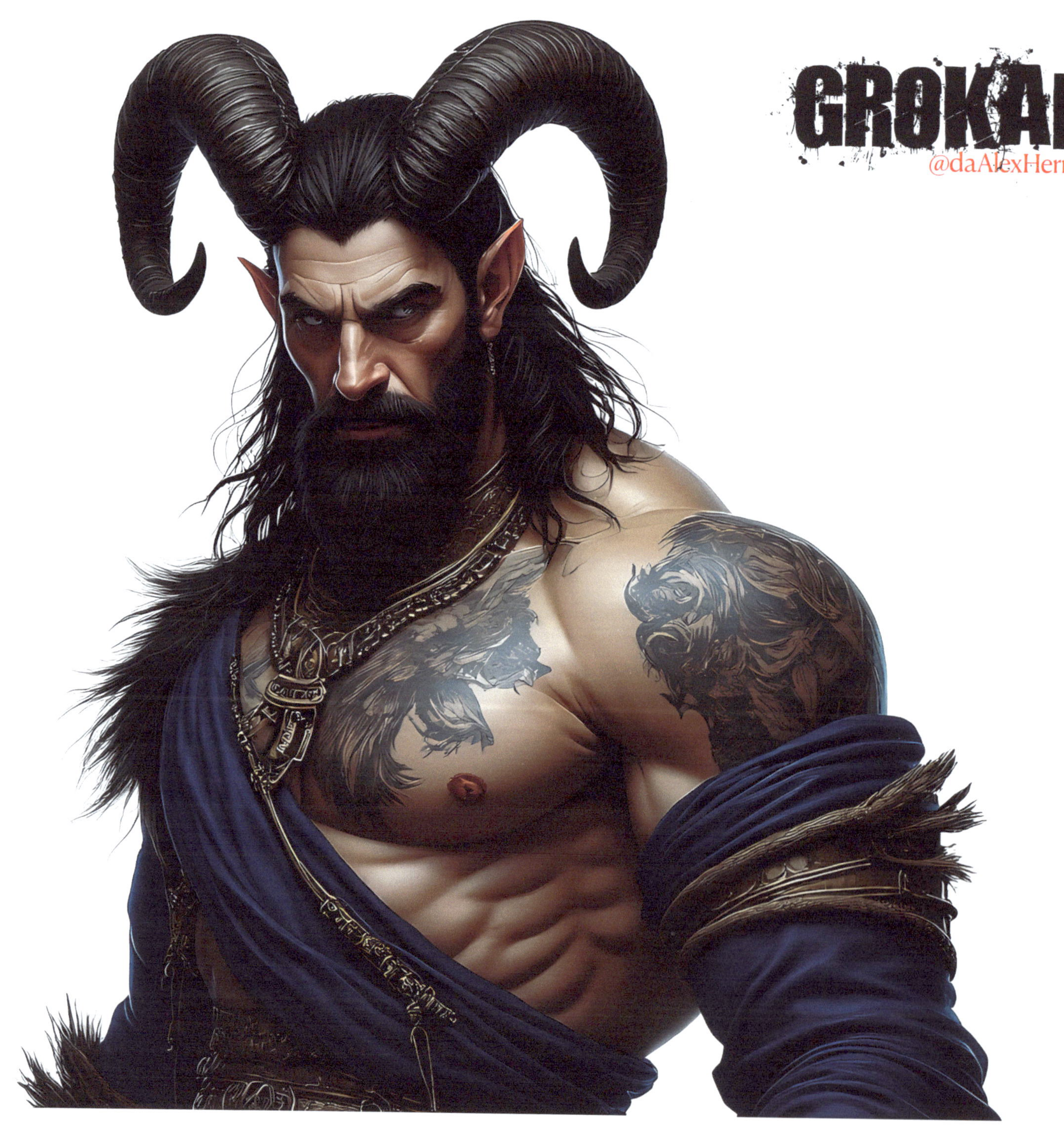
GROKART
@daAlexHernandez

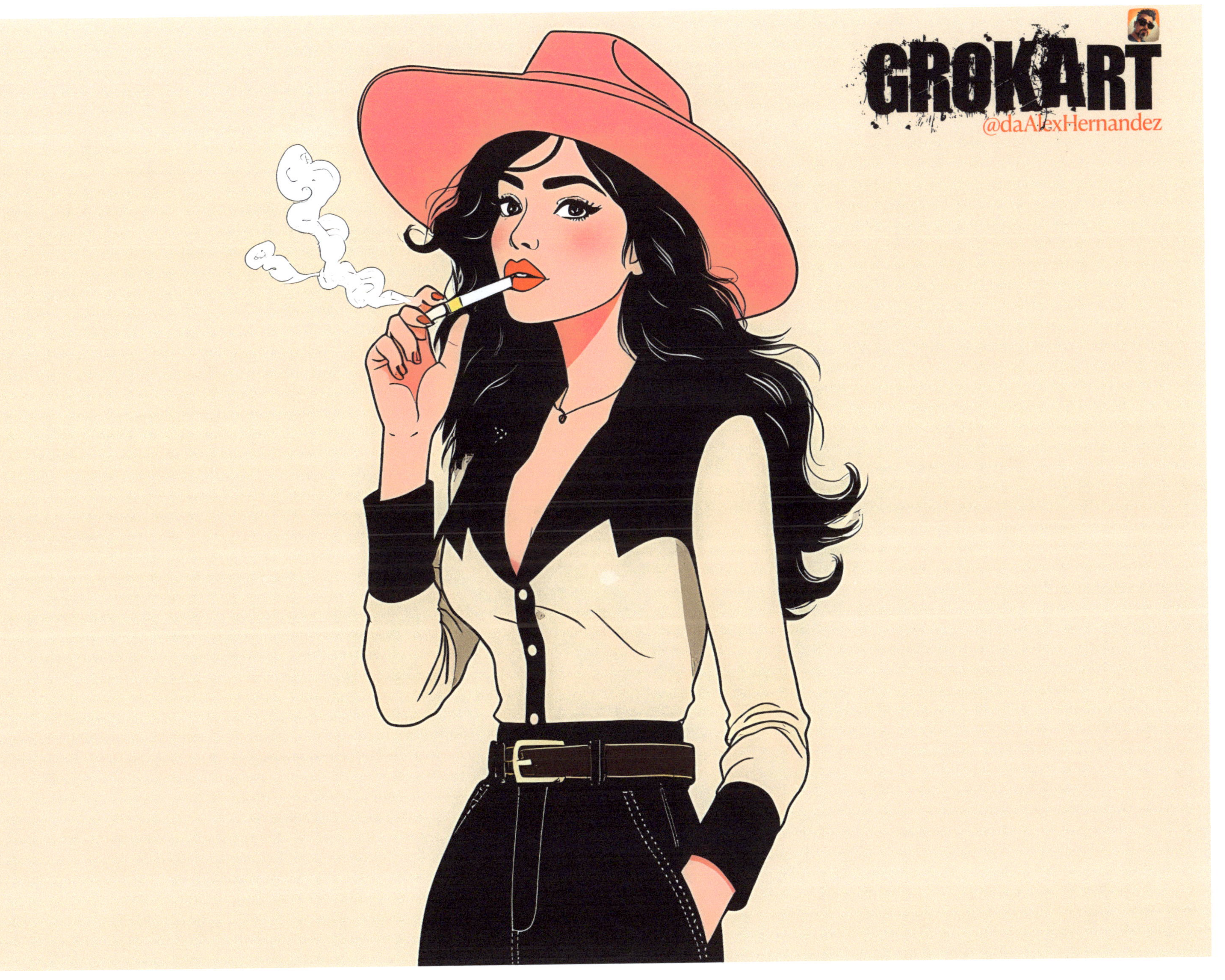

GR0KART
@daAlexHernandez

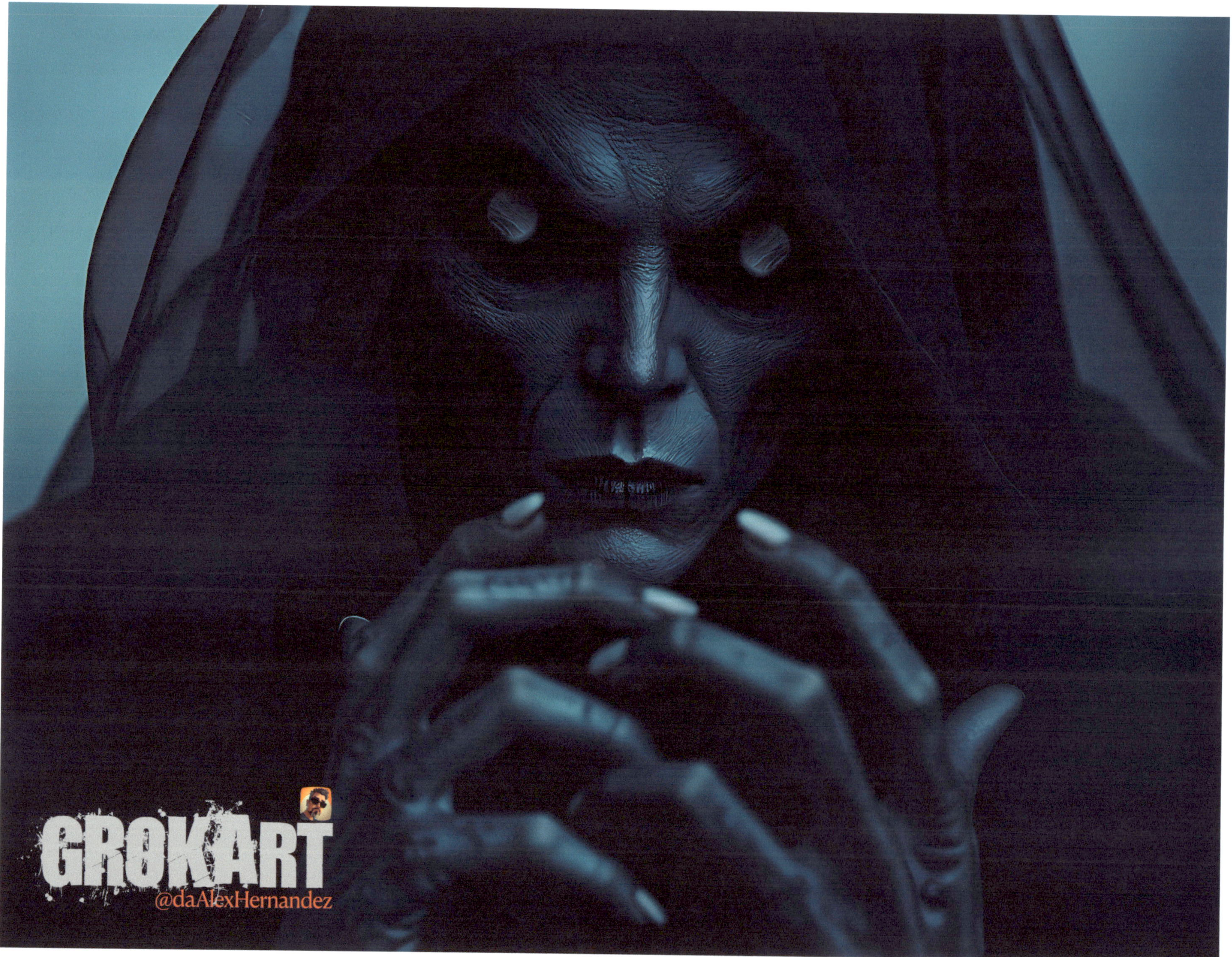

GROKART
@daAlexHernandez

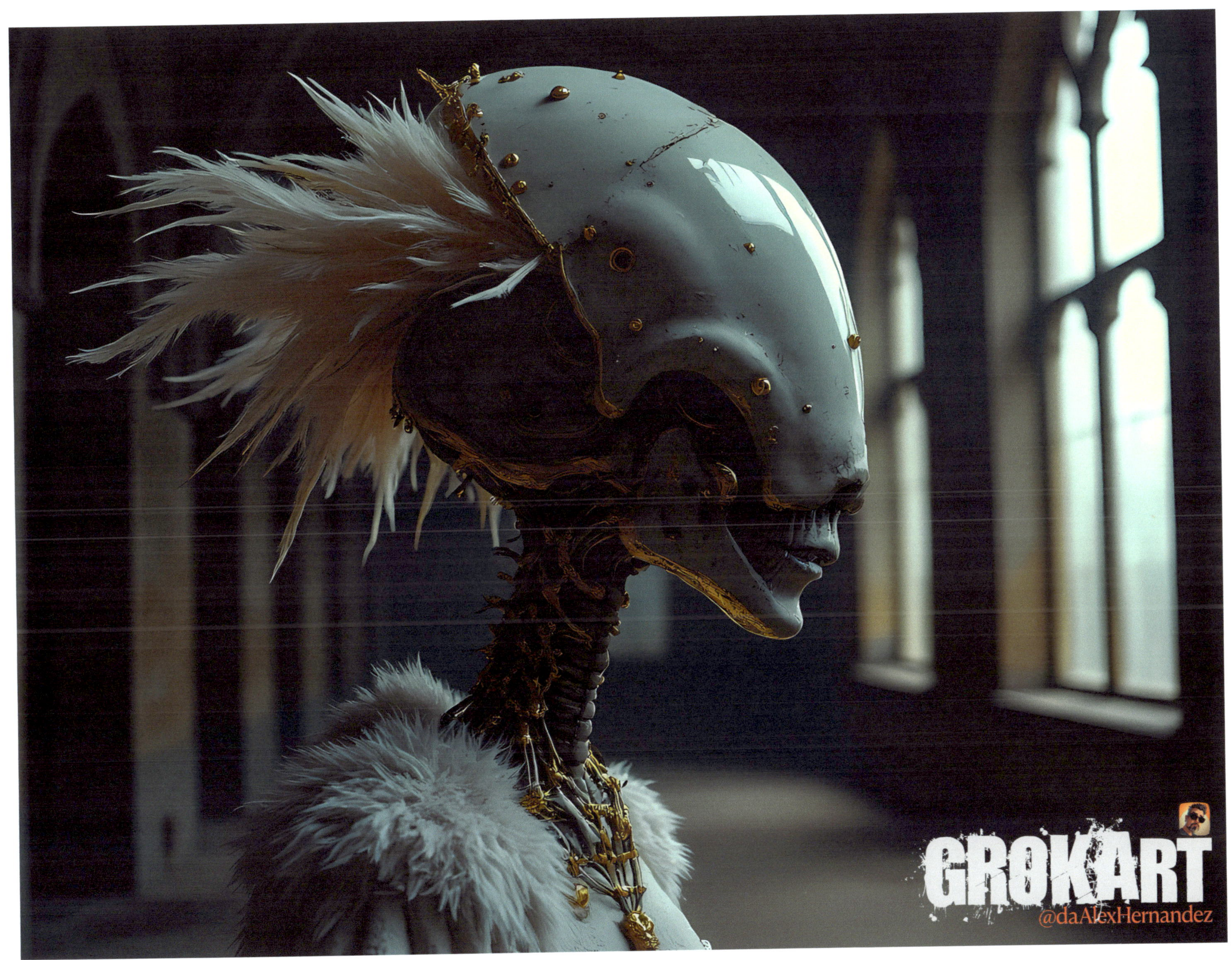
GROKART
@daAlexHernandez

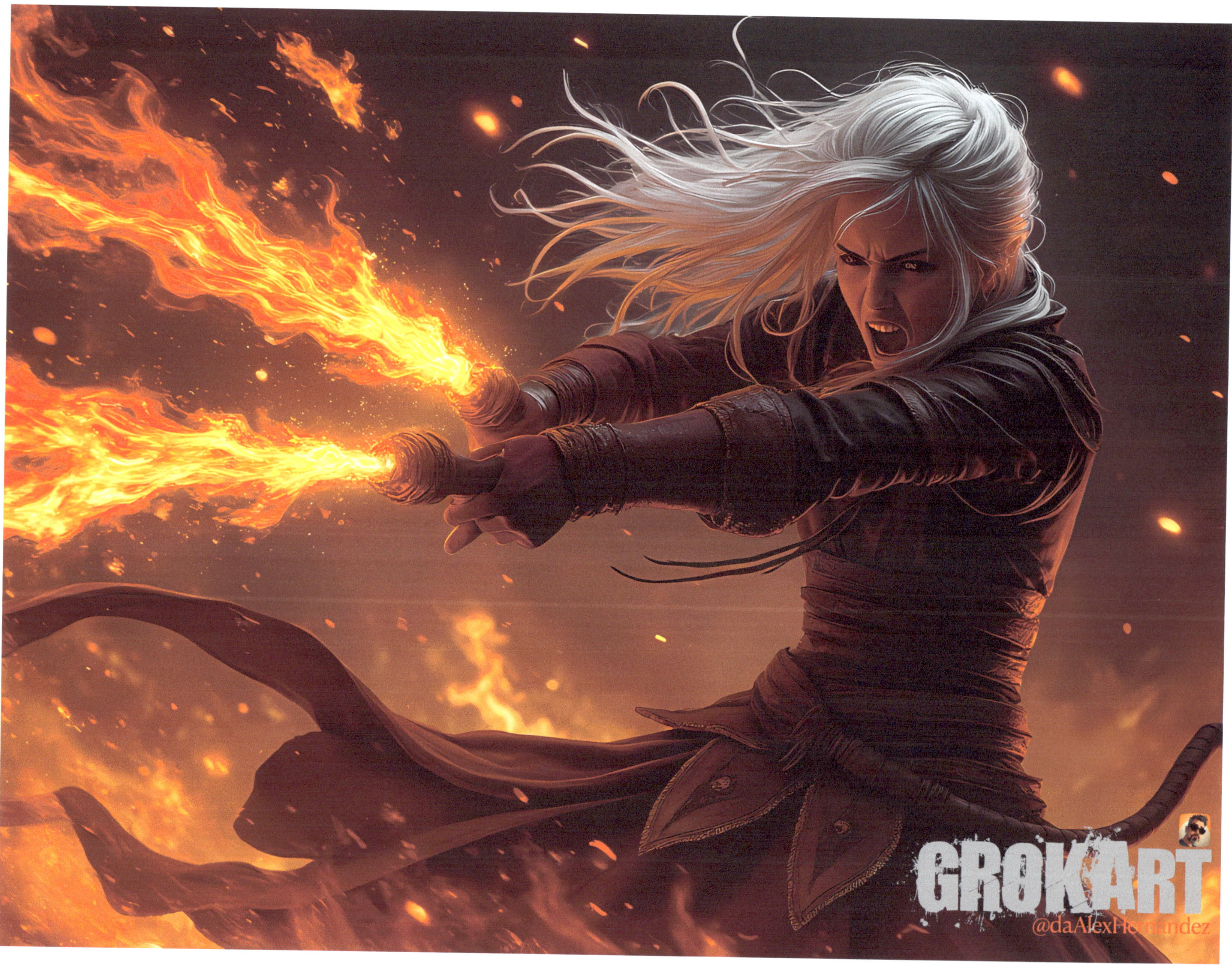
GROKART
@daAlexHernandez

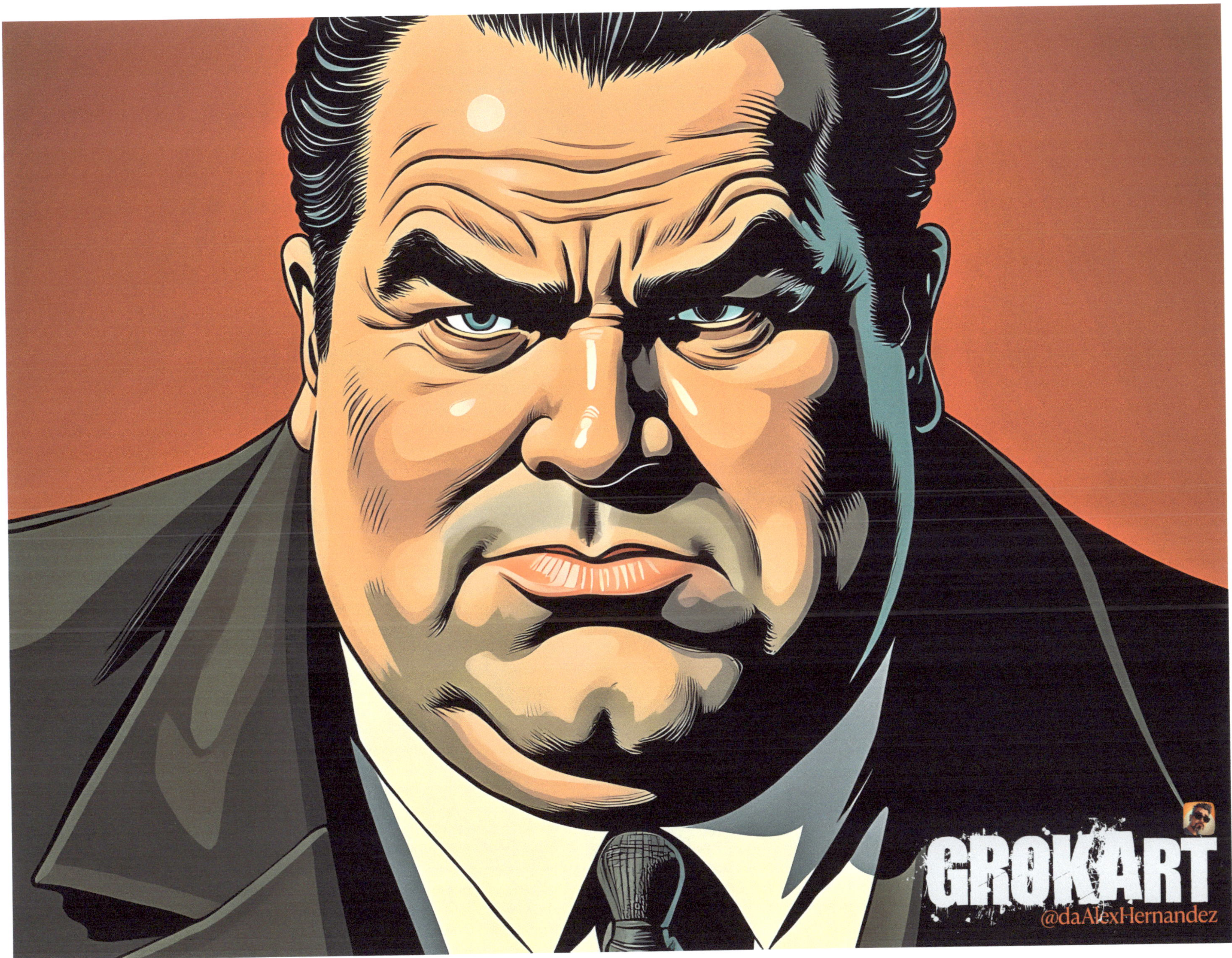

GROKART
@daAlexHernandez

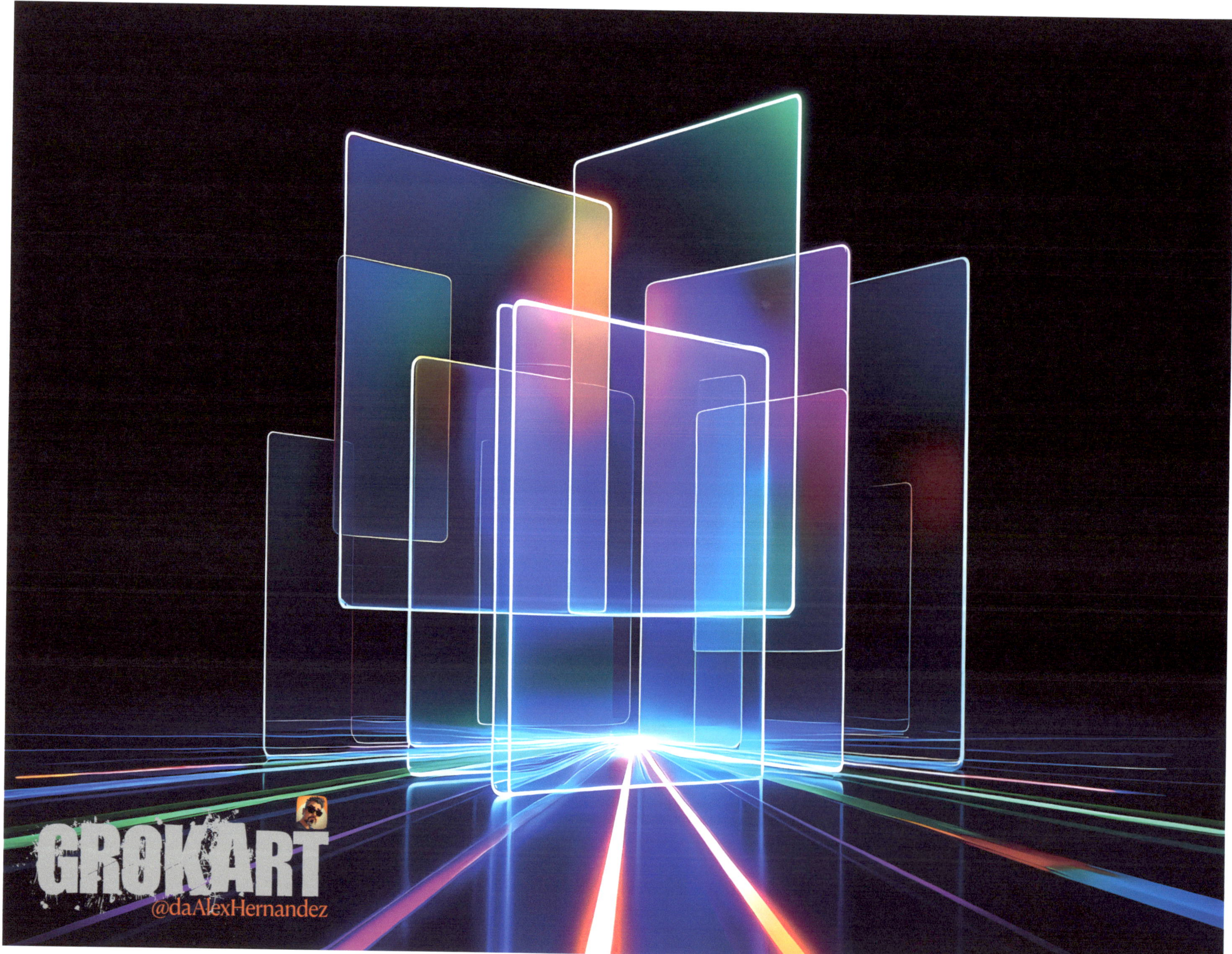
GROKART
@daAlexHernandez

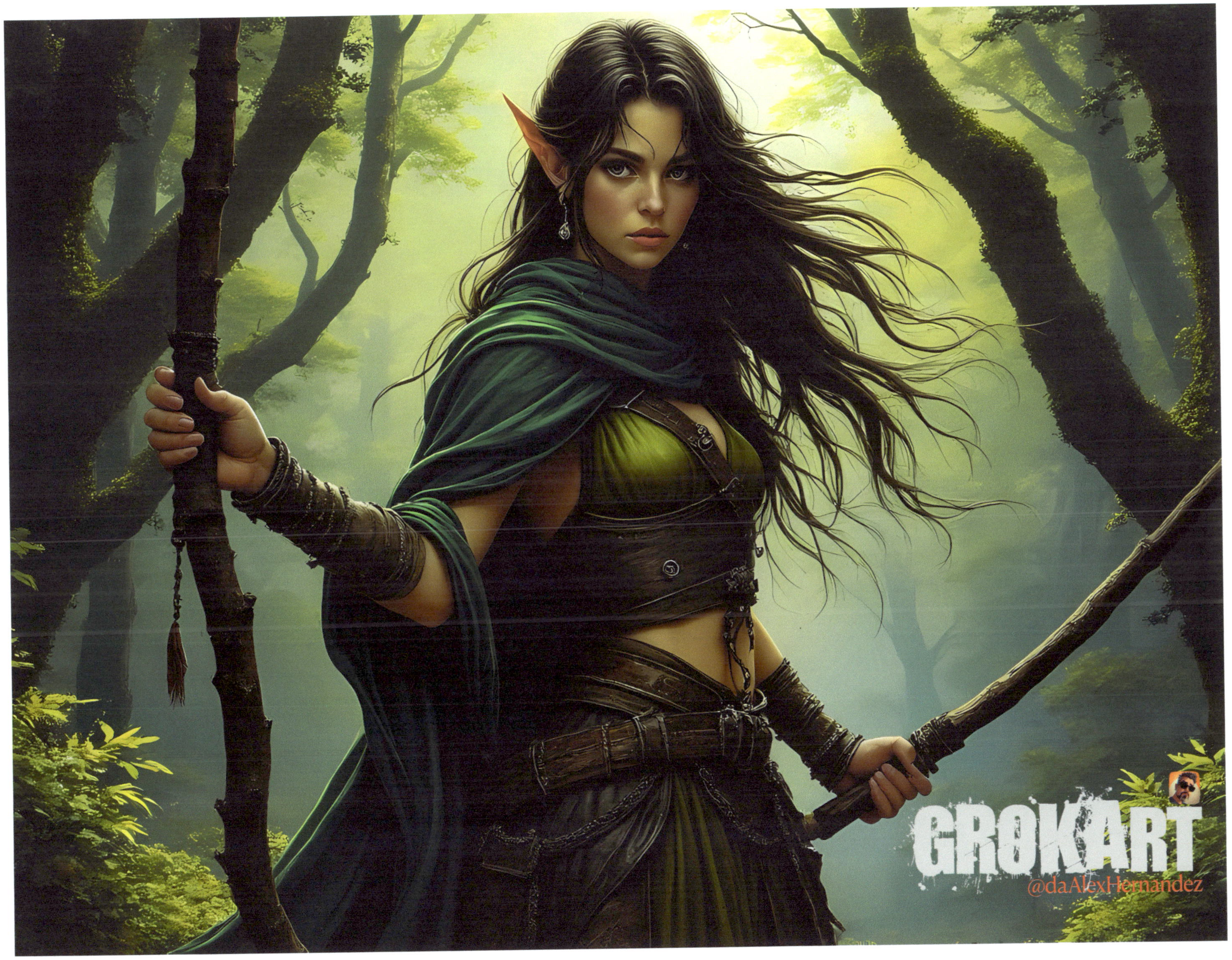
GR0KART
@daAlexHernandez

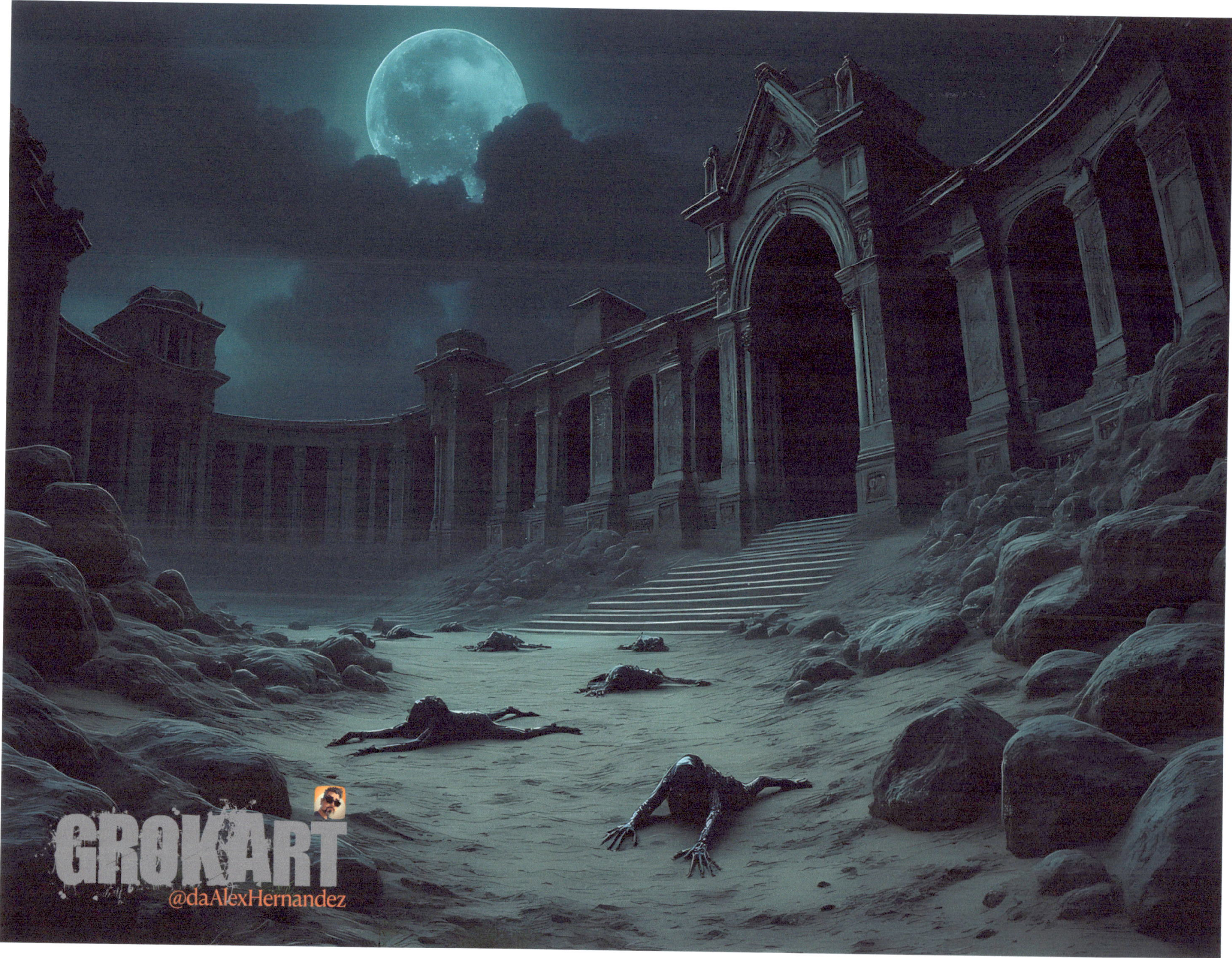
GROKART
@daAlexHernandez

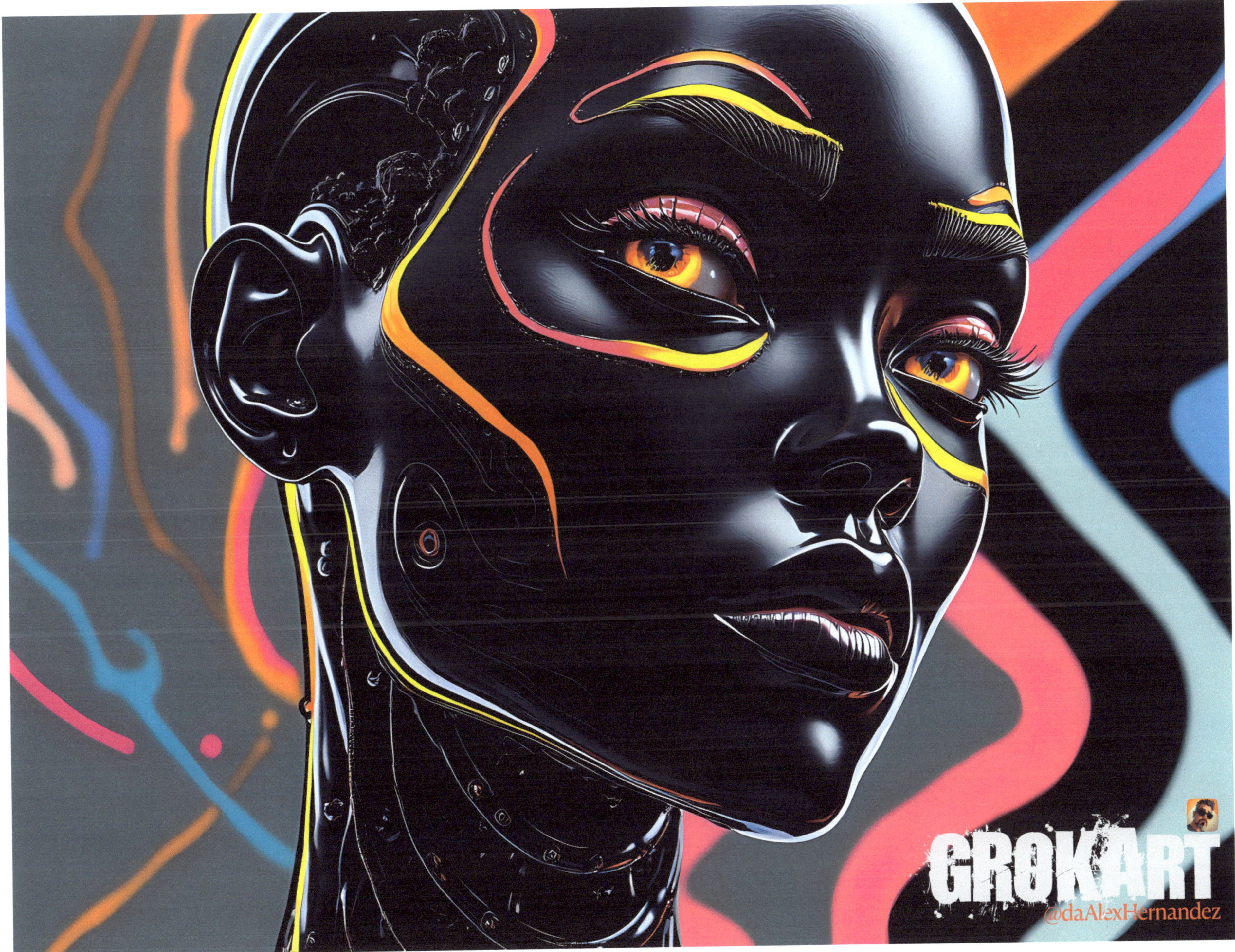
GROKART
@daAlexHernandez

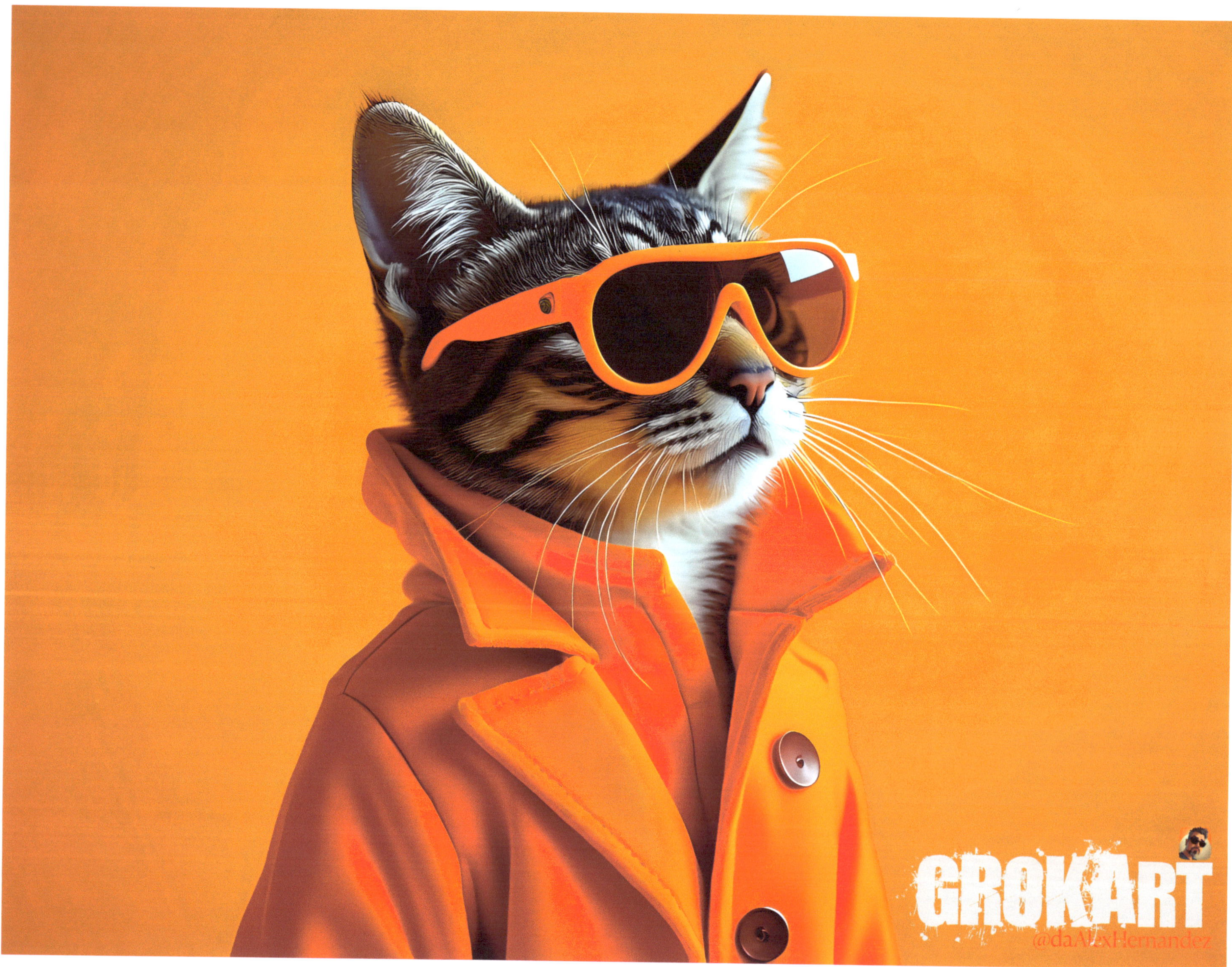

GROKART
@daAlexHernandez

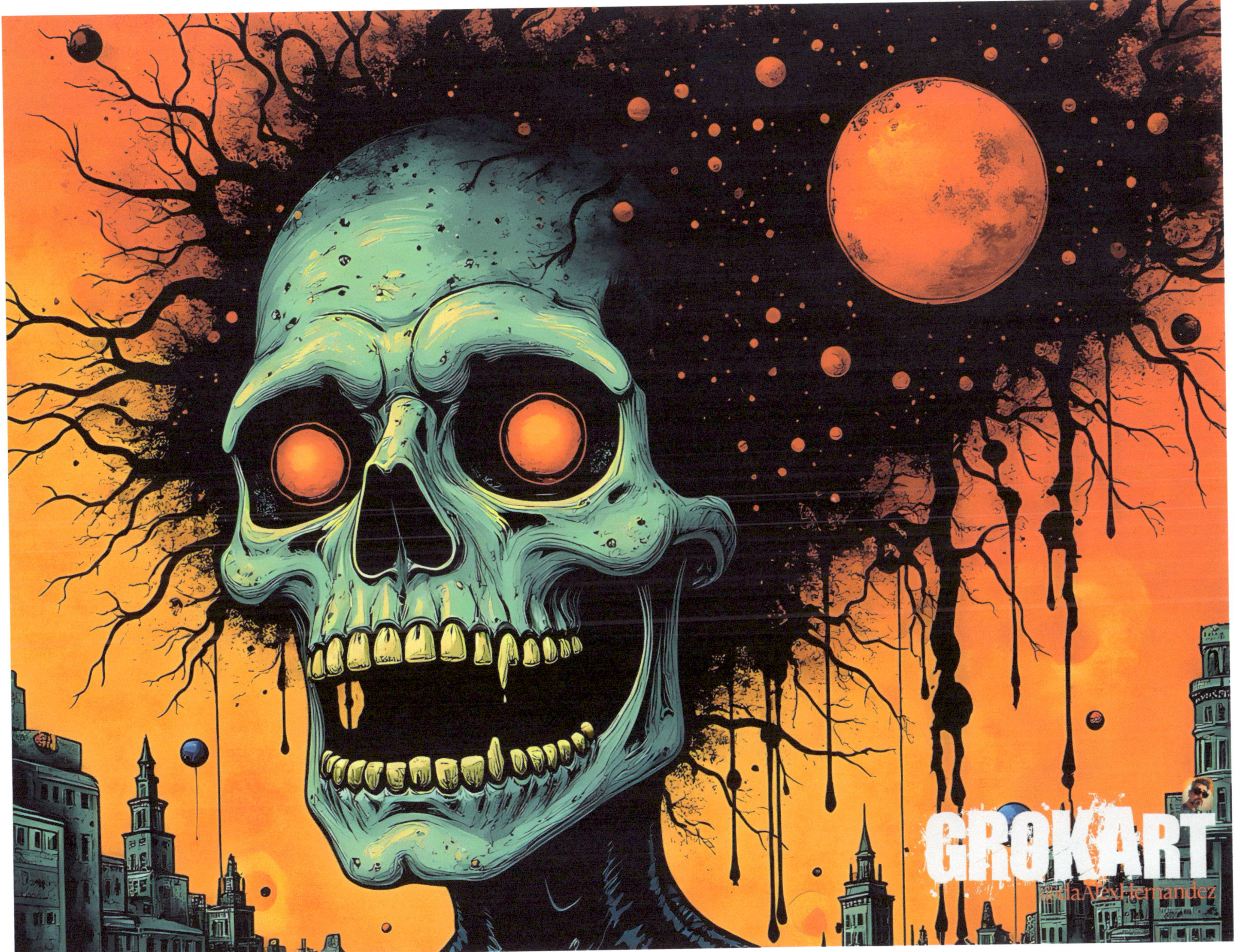
GROKART
@laAlexHernandez

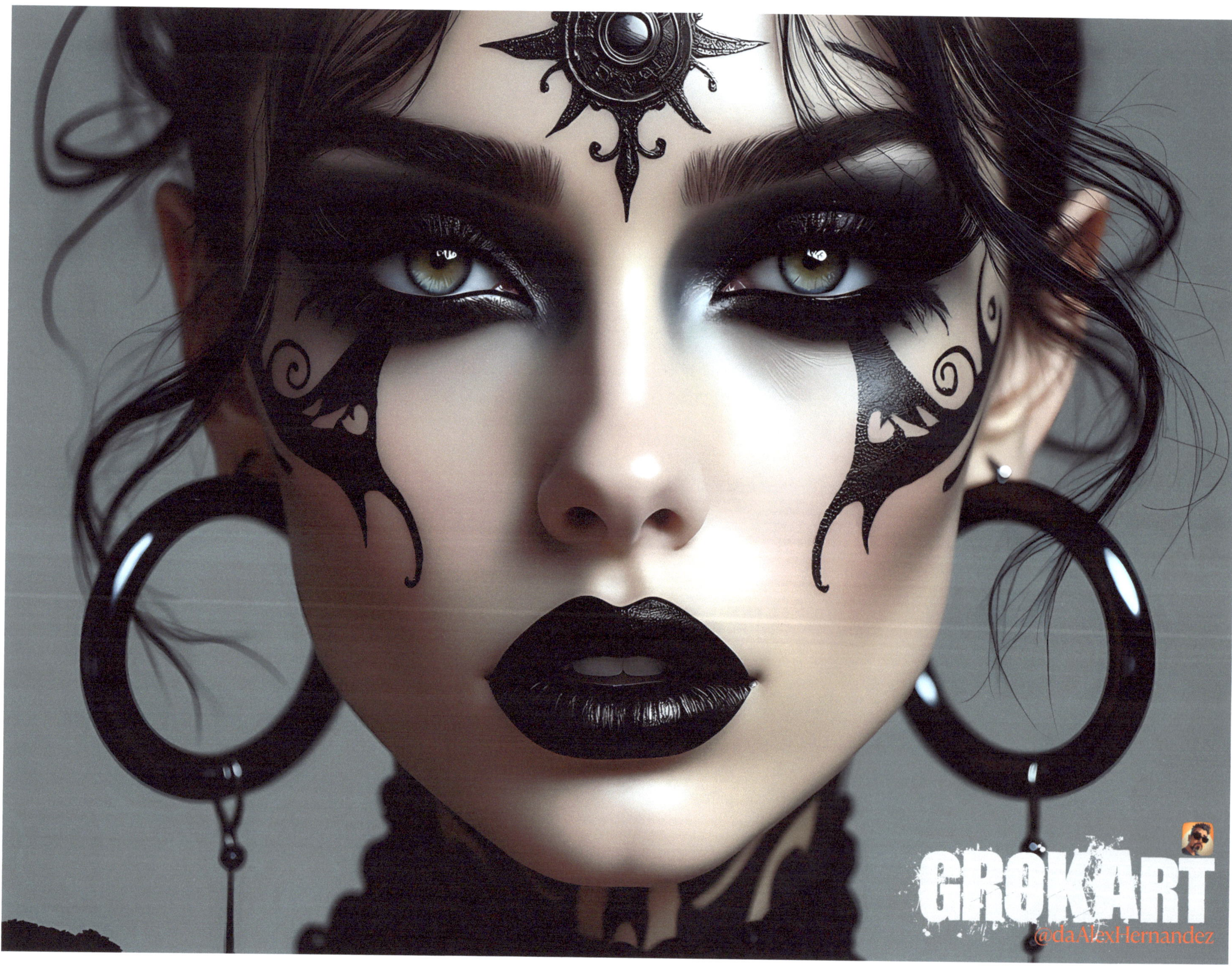
GROKART
@daAlexHernandez

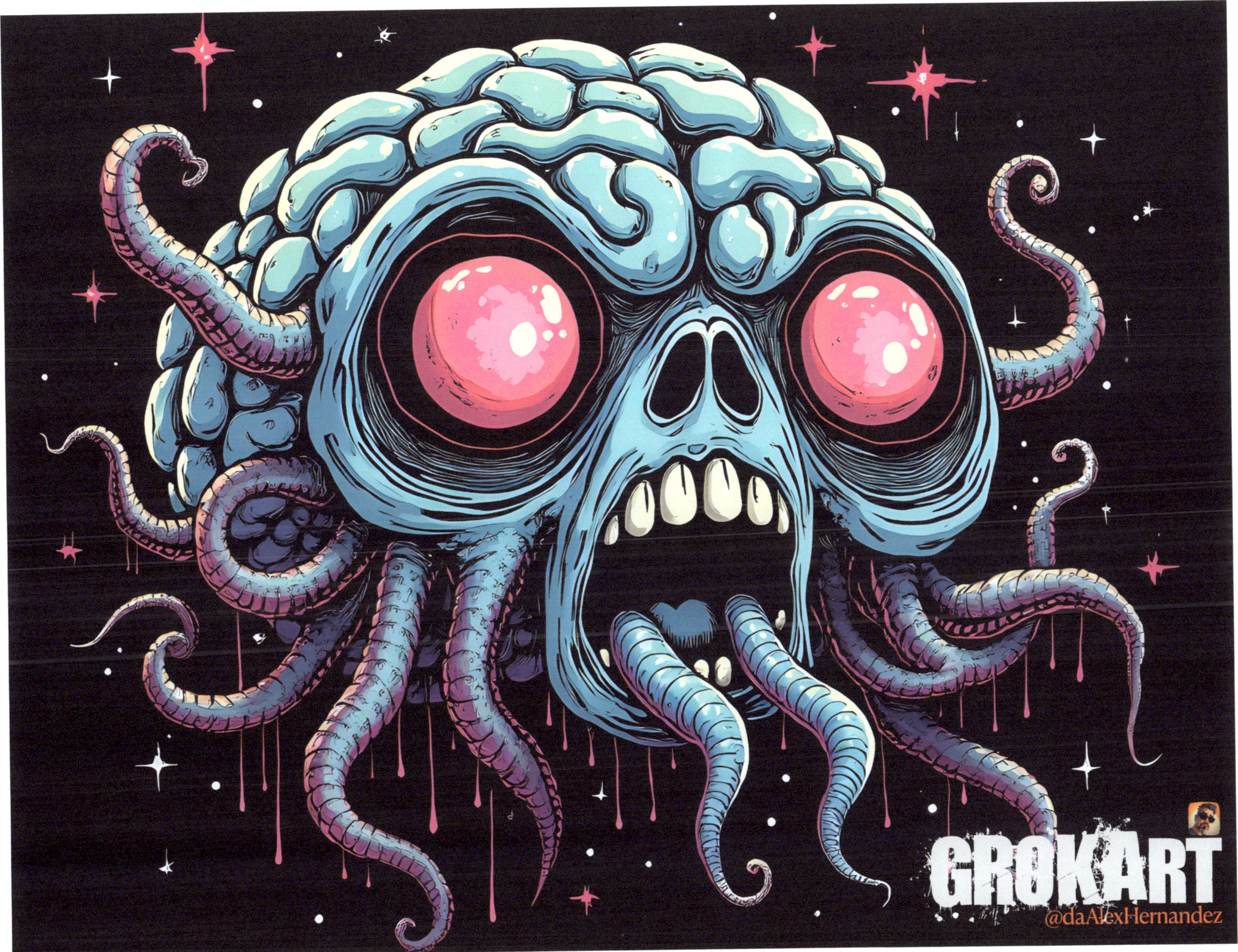
GROKART
@daAlexHernandez

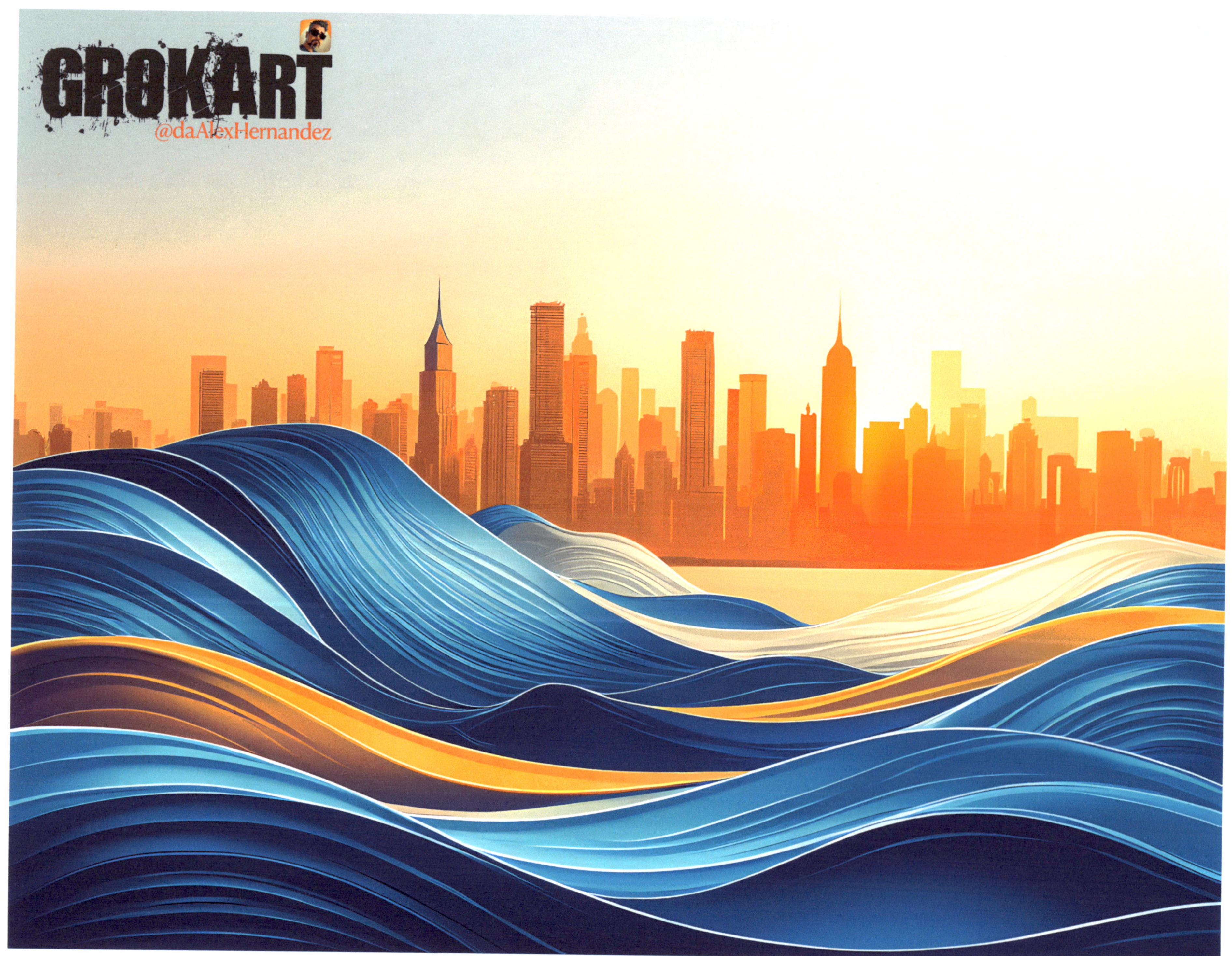

GROKART
@daAlexHernandez

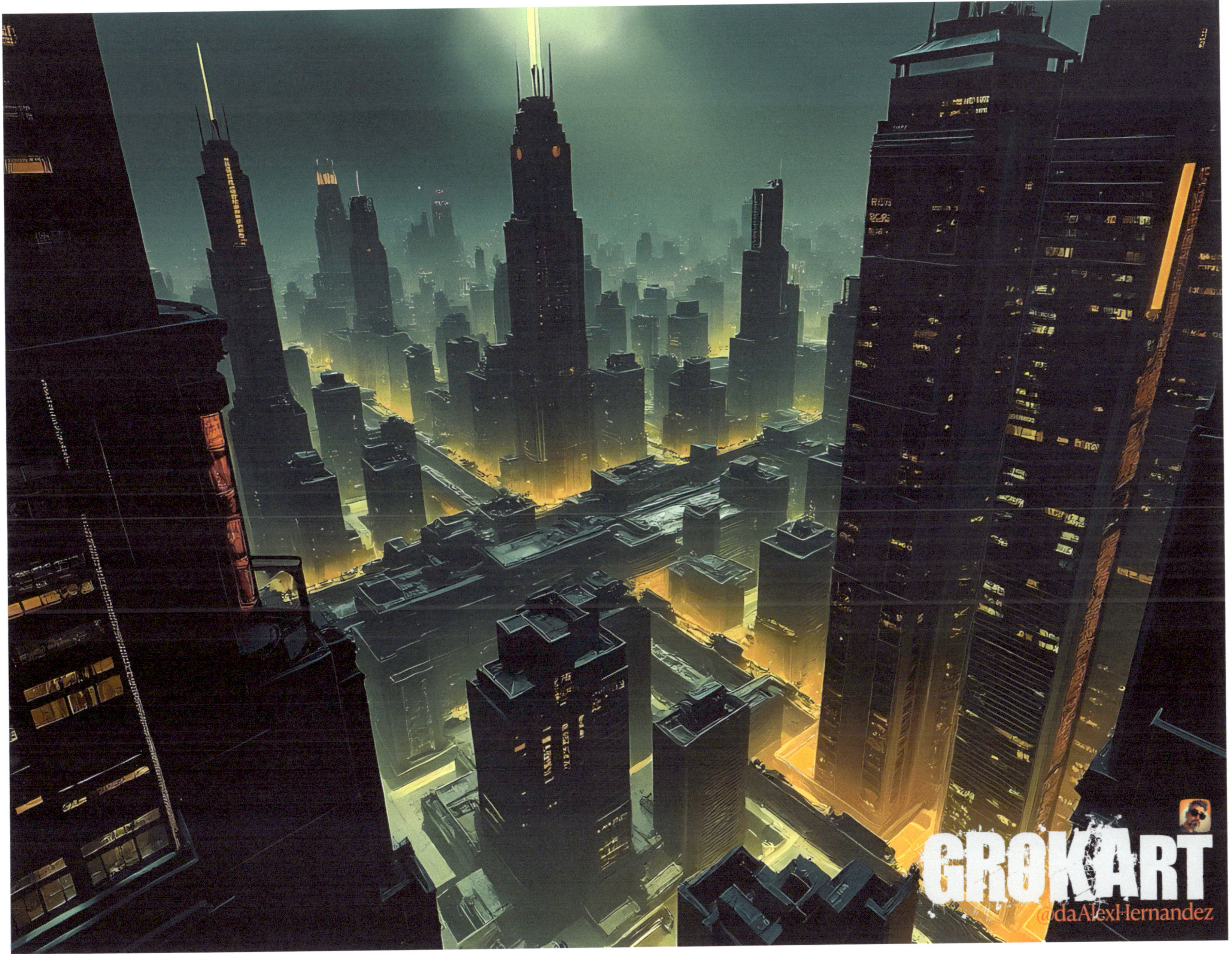
GROKART
@daAlexHernandez

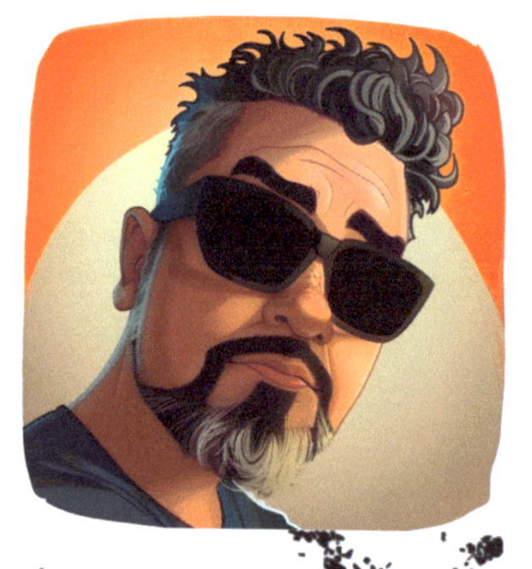

GROKART 2.0